Phillipa Sage worked in the motoring industry for over twenty years, supporting, producing and managing live events for the marketing departments of major motor manufacturers. She went on to become a key member of the production team for *Top Gear Live*. She was also part of the crew who produced *The Grand Tour* for Amazon, working on the pilot and their first film abroad in Jordan. Phillipa went on to have a personal relationship with Jeremy Clarkson and they officially became a couple in 2011. Their relationship ended in 2017. Phillipa is currently moving to Devon, seeking a quieter life with her son Alfie, two dogs, a pony, two Swiss Valais Blacknose sheep, seven ducks, one chicken, one cockerel, one guinea pig and an old Range Rover Vogue. This is her second book after *Off-Road with Clarkson, Hammond & May*.

Also by Phillipa Sage

Off-Road with Clarkson, Hammond & May

THE WONDERFUL WORLD OF

JEREMY CLARKSON

MY LIFE ON THE ROAD WITH JEREMY

PHILLIPA SAGE

First published in 2022 by Ad Lib Publishers Ltd
15 Church Road
London SW13 9HE
www.adlibpublishers.com

Text © 2022 Phillipa Sage

Paperback ISBN 978-1-802470-35-2
eBook ISBN 978-1-802470-91-8

A CIP catalogue record for this book is
available from the British Library.

Printed in the UK
10 9 8 7 6 5 4 3 2 1

For Mum and Dad, Mr and Mrs Sage – thank you.
And my dear Alfie, thank you.

Contents

Preface

Jeremy Who?

Jeremy Clarkson and I first met when he was just thirty-six and a mere twinkle in Amazon's eye. I was a late-blooming twenty-something and was working for an event-management company specialising in the motor industry. I have worked for most of the major motor manufacturers, training their dealers, launching and promoting their new models all over the UK and some of them in Europe.

One of the company's clients was BBC Worldwide Publishing, the commercial arm of the BBC. After an interesting interview process at the BBC, I was chosen and assigned to look after the talent and management backstage at the London International Motor Show.

BBC *Top Gear* back then was hosted by Jeremy, Tiff Needell (who moved on to *Fifth Gear* and has now gone all hip and trendy in his old age and presents a YouTube channel, *Lovecars*) and Quentin Willson, who pops up on TV now and again as a 'motoring expert' and heads up a car-warranty company (a good one – it's paid out on my Range Rover on numerous occasions). Andy Wilman, Jeremy's long-time partner in crime, was the producer. He continues to work alongside his old schoolmate, Clarkson, and produces *The Grand Tour* and *Clarkson's Farm*.

The start of my journey with Mr Clarkson was way before the now infamous trio of Clarkson, Hammond and May conquered the world and became the huge brand that they are now. When I first started working for the BBC and *Top Gear* I didn't know who Jeremy Clarkson was. I had never watched the show on BBC2, (this was before it graduated to BBC1). However, upon getting to know the larger-than-life character, I thought I'd met my soulmate; we were drawn together by childish, schoolboy humour, cars and partying.

Way back then (circa 1996), in the low-budget, dark, smoke- and fume-filled halls of the Earls Court Exhibition Centre and the NEC in Birmingham, the highlights of our nights out were a good curry and gallons of beer followed by ridiculous games of girl-on-girl arm-wrestling, where Richard Hammond reached one of his career highs, playing the part of the table – imagine two girls, leaning over Hammond's mid-section as he tensed his abs as hard as he could. Another after-dinner delight was Celebrity Loo-Roll Challenge, which involved Clarkson, Hammond, May or The Stig having to return from the bathroom with loo roll tucked down their trousers trailing a length of loo paper from cubicle to table without it breaking.

Jeremy was not only the champion of the Celebrity Loo Roll Challenge, but he rapidly ascended to great heights, both in his professional career and his personal life. Our relationship took off too. He swept me off into social circles that most can only dream of, and some have never even thought of.

On one of my first dinner dates with Jeremy, he proclaimed that he'd turned down Madonna to spend the evening with me. He was always out with some famous character from the world of TV, film or media – hardly surprising, as that was his world of work, but I had no idea just how well-connected he was in his personal life.

My working life alongside the notorious motoring journalists became a decadent, never-ending world tour with *Top Gear Live* in private jets, helicopters and superyachts, which I have written about in detail in my first book, *Off-Road with Clarkson, Hammond and May*. (Here's as good a place as any to get a plug in.) Girl-on-girl arm-wrestling over Richard Hammond in a Birmingham curry house turned into girl-throwing into swimming pools, with the furthest throw winning. Coffee in polystyrene cups and Family Circle biscuits transformed into champagne and caviar.

Clarkson led a life which straddled the low budgets of BBC TV production to touring the world with the blow-the-budget arena show *Top Gear Live*, and a social life with some of the most powerful, famous and wealthy people in the world.

Once we were officially a couple, my first taste of Jeremy's inner circle was a party at a British aristocrat's London residence. We spent numerous weekends at Jemima Khan's country estate and partied and holidayed with media moguls, members of parliament, including prime ministers, film stars, pop stars, directors and producers, lords and ladies, even royalty. There were no polystyrene cups or dingy backstage smoking dens. We dined at the top tables, drank the finest wine, flew first class all the way, and holidayed on private islands.

I was honoured and humbled to be accepted into this exclusive, privileged world, coming from such humble beginnings as I had done. I had found myself in the extraordinary world of Jeremy Clarkson.

Introduction

Life in the Fast Lane

Have you ever wondered at a certain point in your life, 'How did I get here?' Jeremy and I had those thoughts and asked that question on numerous occasions, literally all around the world. One such occasion was when I arranged, for Jeremy's Christmas present, a private viewing of a Turner Exhibition at Tate Britain. Jeremy loved art, but to try to visit a popular London gallery full of tourists would be a nightmare for him, as it would also be for other visitors who were not Clarkson fans, since those frantic to get a selfie with him would bump into those who can't bear his bombastic, opinionated ways. Let's face it, he's very Marmite: there are just as many who support him as those who do not.

Anywhere with a large number of members of the general public is a bit of a nightmare for the big man, and anyone close to him. It's a bit of an irony that how Jeremy presents himself as his TV persona encourages fans to behave in a similar way. They noisily charge across an airport or street shouting, 'JEZZA!', desperate for an autograph or to engage in a debate over their favourite car and, of course, to stick a phone in his face and grab a selfie. What I call 'The Real Jeremy Clarkson' hates this with a passion. Believe it or not, he hates being famous, but has clearly become comfortable with the trimmings fame brings.

So, I had arranged with the lovely people at Tate Britain, in return for a donation to the museum, to have an hour or so to ourselves before the public were allowed in. As we pulled up in the car park at the back entrance to the museum, in a Ferrari (just to top it off) Jeremy said, 'I bet you didn't see this coming?' He was right and the soon-to-be repeated question of, 'How did I get here?' popped into my mind, too.

All the adventures and extraordinary events with which I am – hopefully – about to entertain you were never in my wildest dreams. Although I felt extremely lucky to experience such fun and luxury – and I defy anyone not to get excited at the opportunity to fly in a private jet or holiday on a private island. To be honest, I longed for a more normal life with the man who I thought of as 'my best friend', someone to cook a roast with for all our family and slob out on the sofa with, watching the footy or a movie, to read the Sunday papers with over breakfast and share life's highs and lows with.

Jeremy often said that he longed for an empty diary and to just potter around our planned vegetable plot at the farm. However, he has an addictive personality (that probably won't surprise you, some of the evidence is right there in that large belly of his!). His foremost addiction, though, is work. His second is play!

As could happen to any of us, I got caught in the fast lane of life, more like a German autobahn in this case, and with the most famous fast driver in the world. It became increasingly difficult to pull over for a break.

1

First Dates

My first nights out with Jeremy were simple dinners at his favourite curry house in Fulham or Notting Hill. Sometimes we would go to celebrity haunts such as Pharmacy in Notting Hill, where I remember rubbing shoulders with intriguing characters such as Salman Rushdie and Mariella Frostrup. Once, when dining there, we were seated next to Matthew Wright, then showbiz gossip columnist for the *Daily Mirror*. There was a crowd of us from the *Top Gear* crew from the London Motor Show, including quite a few glamorous girls. Jeremy had a quiet word with Matthew to make sure we didn't end up in his next column. Other favourite haunts were celebrity chef of the moment Antony Worrall Thompson's restaurant, Notting Grill, where Jezza could enjoy some traditional meat and two veg, and E&O, where we were seated next to *Jurassic Park* star Sam Neale, and enjoyed some pan-Asian delights.

Wherever we went, Jeremy was not only recognised as a celebrity, but it seemed he knew everyone in London Town personally – well, certainly in all the hip places to be. These dinners were often tagged on to the end of a long day's work and were nothing more than two colleagues going out for a bite to eat, although Jeremy is a terrible flirt and appeared to love showing off his interesting, famous, powerful and influential acquaintances to me, around town.

Obviously, we got on and Jeremy began to demand my presence more and more. I wondered if he was trying to impress me by taking me to exciting places and name-dropping who he'd been partying with of late. When he told me he'd turned down dinner with Madonna to have dinner with me, I was not impressed; I was only ever flattered that a man of such intelligence, who was so busy, wanted to spend time with me. And I really enjoyed his company. In the motor industry we knew a lot of the same people and we were never short of something to talk about.

In those early days, he (though you may struggle to believe this) was a great mentor to me; he can be very wise and was supportive of me when I was struggling to get back to work after a physical and mental breakdown. We had a great laugh over the fact that I had weekly magnesium injections; he suggested I just eat a Ford Focus gearbox – apparently that's what they are made of.

*　*　*　*

Jeremy suggested we were kindred spirits, 'meant to be', as we had both started life in a relatively humble way in fairly typical working-class families, coincidentally, in houses beside the A1(M), just a few hundred miles apart; Jeremy in Doncaster, and me in Welwyn, Hertfordshire. We had both enjoyed playing in woodlands, making camps and looking after our pet guinea pigs, like many normal kids in the olden days.

Despite our common ground and similarities, as I'm sure you are aware, Jeremy does like taking risks and I do not. I was dead against going to some restaurant opening in the West

End where he said there would be a lot of people who knew him. We were in the midst of a full-blown affair by this time. However, Jeremy is very persuasive, shall we say, and we were soon stepping out of a cab and bumping into Sir Bob Geldof, who Jeremy stopped to have a chat with, introducing me as a work colleague, which of course I was.

Inside this huge restaurant and club – the Atlantic or Titanic, I think, it's all a bit blurry as I was nervous and it's a long time ago – I was soon being introduced to great British aristocrats such as Lord Edward Spencer Churchill, who is related both to Sir Winston Churchill and to Princess Diana, and rock-'n'-roll royalty like Nick Mason from Pink Floyd and his actress wife, Nettie.

We also had more low-key evenings, when he took me to his favourite pubs and simple restaurants along Wandsworth Bridge Road, but even then, we would always bump into someone extraordinary like Lord Brocket, who is from my neck of the woods in Hertfordshire. Lord Brocket had recently got out of prison having been convicted of committing insurance fraud. According to reports, some of his cars, including Ferraris, had been dismantled and some of the parts buried in the grounds of Brocket Hall. Not your average back garden – he had over 500 acres in which to dig a big enough hole to hide his classic car collection. That would have been an awesome find for a metal detectorist!

We also had a lot of nights out with the *Top Gear Live* crew when we were working together, which I've written about in my other book (*Off-Road with Clarkson, Hammond and May*, another little plug!). Some of the same crew worked on the TV show too, so whilst still under cover as 'the other woman' it was perfectly feasible for me to be invited to some of the TV-crew parties, which were nowhere near as glamorous as our *World Tour* shenanigans, but just as much fun.

* * * *

Two of those parties were epic. The first, I remember, started out in a rather dingy, though hip, bar in Shoreditch, which at first Mr Clarkson was most disgruntled about. Firstly, because, in his opinion, it was not in London. Anything not in Notting Hill, Fulham, Chelsea or the right part of central London was not London, and not worth visiting, according to Clarkson. Secondly, because this incredibly trendy bar, in which we had a private room, was poorly lit, was uncarpeted and the drinks were served in plastic cups. His lordship was not impressed.

However, after enough drinks to blur the bar's inadequacies and some other party treats, Jeremy began to enjoy himself. His mood, and the party, got way better when someone discovered a door linking us to another private party, which turned out to be Simon Pegg's and Nick Frost's production company's. Their room had a bowling alley! The two parties merged and it was soon discovered that bowling fuelled by alcohol is a lot of fun until your girlfriend (me) is doing rather well at it and getting a lot of attention. Then it's time to leave.

The following year, if I remember rightly, the budget was blown a little, or someone at the BBC got a good deal, or maybe Andy Wilman decided to make sure the big man was happy with the location. Whatever, this quite ridiculous evening in central London started in a private room with the added benefit of a roof terrace for smokers. Obviously, this was a big bonus for Jeremy, who was known to do eighty a day when stressed out on a demanding schedule, as he so often was. As the night went on, Jeremy and James (I don't think Richard was there) ventured down to the public bar, in search of more fags, I think. I followed and, yet again, we merged with someone else's festive night out, *The One Show*'s.

At that time, Chris Evans was hosting it with Alex Jones. They were both at the bar drinking cocktails. Jeremy and James got chatting and I was introduced to everyone. I was intrigued by the delicious-looking cocktails Chris and Alex had. I had never seen anything like them before: a dark, chocolatey colour with a cream-coloured, slightly frothy top. 'What are they?' I asked. Chris jumped in and said I should try one, they were espresso martinis. Mr Evans swiftly ordered me one. As I had already sunk quite a lot of alcohol, I thought, 'What a great idea! Something to wake me up.' The cocktail was fantastic and I was soon on to my second, which led smoothly to my third.

Sometime later, we were all heading to a nightclub, led by Chris, who I can confirm is like the Pied Piper of partying and a deft promoter of alcohol. I can now also recollect that Richard was there – I think. Arghh! I have had a lot of nights out with these guys with a lot of alcohol and these occasions do tend to be a bit blurry, literally. However, what I do remember was Chris coming back from the bar with a huge tray of multi-coloured shots, which he gifted to us all, gleefully handing them out with a wicked smile on his face.

I know we all danced and bumped into each other a lot on the dance-floor and then I remember wobbling downstairs with Jeremy and James. James literally fell out of the entrance and Jeremy and I had to help him to stand upright. To be honest, I don't think I was much help. I then remember hailing cabs, one for James and the other for Jeremy and me and then everything went black.

The next morning, as I crawled into the bathroom, I saw my dress and boots on the floor. My dress was silk and embellished with sparkly things, and my boots were suede; now, they were both decorated with vomit. I couldn't face them, so I put them into separate plastic bags to be taken home and dealt with later.

You can probably feel the headache I had, though whatever you're imagining, please note that it was much worse than you could possibly imagine. Jeremy had had to pull himself together and drive to one of his children's schools for a meeting or concert or something. I could not move from the bathroom or bed until the evening.

I couldn't face my boots for a whole year. I got them home and left them in a corner by my washing machine. I was ashamed and didn't want to face the hideous mess, nor the reality that I had probably totally ruined my boots.

What I did have to face was a hideous mess which I discovered over a day later, when looking for a lip gloss in the handbag I had used for our Christmas night out. I found, to my horror, that, I believe in an effort not to spoil the taxi we were in, I'd thrown up in my handbag!! The lesson here is: DO NOT go out drinking with Chris Evans. Unfortunately/fortunately, I did so on several occasions, but more about that later.

Perhaps Jeremy's favourite most famous person of all was Princess Diana. He delighted in ogling her as she arrived at the gym in Fulham, in her Audi convertible. The gym was conveniently just next door to his flat, which was high enough up for him not to be spotted staring out of the window, but did give him a great view of the perfectly formed princess in her gym gear. I must admit I too loved to be that close to Diana, whom I idolised (and, very weirdly, have been mistaken for when I was on a trip in South Korea, but that's a whole other story).

As the years passed, I realised it was Jeremy who was excited by the people he mixed with and constantly rubbing shoulders with celebrity. He was the one who couldn't get enough of parties and dinners, especially when they were attended by glamorous girls like Kate Moss, Uma Thurman, Jemima Khan and his old favourite, Kristin Scott Thomas. I, on the other hand, have always been fascinated by people, full stop – whether they are the Queen or the dustman. I love people and am always fascinated by what makes them tick. I don't care who you are as far as social standing goes. You are either a nice person who I'd like to hang out with, or you're not.

2

Out Out

Once we were outed by the *Mirror*, reportedly sleeping above Richard Hammond in a corner suite in the Ritz, in Norway. (I love the way the tabloids' descriptive writing knows no bounds. Can you imagine how Richard Hammond felt when he found out he'd been sleeping right underneath us?!) After a lot of trauma, mainly for poor Jeremy's long-suffering wife and children, we started to venture out as an official couple and Jeremy introduced me, in his own words, to his 'Weird World'.

Jeremy was nervous about launching me into his inner circle; he told me he didn't want anyone to be mean to me. But if you hang around the almighty Mr Clarkson long enough, you learn it's all about him and I think he was terrified of being judged and me not fitting in with his high and mighty friends. After all, I had started my working life as a mere hairdresser. JC never wanted me to mention that; well, not until he found it very useful for me to cut his hair on demand, reportedly better than anyone else could. (Said just to keep me sweet, I'm sure.)

He tested the water with what he thought was a safe bet, a private party just down the road from his penthouse flat in

Holland Park. The host was Tom Astor, a minor aristocrat, who I can't find on Wikipedia, which would have helped me to fill you in a bit more on this loveable rogue. Jeremy enjoyed the fact that most of his friends were easily found on Google, and even looked up certain acquaintances prior to arriving at their parties so he had inside info to help initiate conversations, or to make sure he didn't put his foot in it when expressing one of his strong opinions.

What I do know about Tom is that he is the brother of Rose van Cutsem, née Astor, and her husband Hugh is best friends with Princes William and Harry. Rose and Hugh's daughter was one of William and Kate's bridesmaids, the most notorious one, who leant over the balcony at Buckingham Palace, pulling a disgruntled face and covering her ears. The Astor family are not only friends with the royals, they are also related in some complicated way that I'm not going to explain here, partly because I don't think I can. I learnt it was very difficult to know who was related to whom with a lot of the high society peeps, as not only were they often the issue of multiple marriages but they also had many different titles and names.

Of course, the Astors are also famous for their involvement in the Profumo Affair at Cliveden, a tale of hedonistic parties and political scandal back in the sixties. And here I was, about to be launched into the modern-day version of this self-same hedonistic world, at this point, very naively. I could never have imagined who or what I was going to encounter in the tumultuous years that followed.

On this particular evening, Jeremy briefed me on Tom's life and the connections as described above, which all sounded fascinating, but all I was concerned about was how I would be received as 'the other woman' and whether I would be able to contribute to, and keep up, with the many conversations between all these extraordinary people.

It was a lovely summer's evening and a rare treat to walk along the street arm in arm with my man, beneath blossom-filled trees. Ooh, God, I've gone all Mills & Boon. To be honest, this collection of stories will often read more like a Jilly Cooper tale – I met her too.

We arrived at a pretty Georgian townhouse nestled in amongst the trees of a very desirable street in Holland Park. It was actually rather unkempt, which surprised me, but I found it comforting that even the friends/relatives of the royal family can't keep up with their gardening. I found it rather endearing, intriguing and less intimidating as an entrance.

We were soon welcomed by Tom, a classic aristo – well-spoken, almost plummy, good head of hair, open-collared shirt and jeans, bumptiously welcoming us in and offering us champagne. We were then led through to the back garden, which really was an oasis – a charming secret garden in the heart of West London. Unkempt like the front of the house, but filled with rambling roses and blossoming trees and shrubs.

In the middle of this charming scene, a long table – about thirty feet long, if I remember rightly – was dressed with a pretty linen tablecloth, fresh flowers and candles. Once seated, we were served a delicious three-course meal by smartly dressed staff, accompanied by constant and free-flowing top-ups of booze. It was idyllic.

It wasn't long before I felt very much at home, enjoying the banter of my fellow diners. As often happens with me, I was surrounded by men. As you might imagine, having worked in such a male-dominated industry, I am like one of the boys. I'm not one to gossip with the girls, admiring shoes and handbags. I just like a laugh when I'm out. Interestingly, and slightly unnervingly, at this point I think it was me who was the topic of the gossip amongst the ladies, so I was feeling slightly uncomfortable. I felt even more so when I learnt that the chap sitting next to me made porn films in Amsterdam, or some other sex capital of the world. He was quite an eccentric, dressed in a light-coloured suit topped off with a cravat. I would guess he was in his early forties and he was a party pro. Happily offering drugs and encouraging the takers.

Drugs and drink were quite a big feature in this scene, but I shall set the record straight now by saying that I have only ever had a lightly laced cookie, in my early twenties, that did nothing for me and, apart from that seemingly pointless activity, I don't get on terribly well with alcohol although I've tried so hard! So I've always been wary of taking drugs. As I've said, I do like a laugh and to me getting drunk is fun as long as you don't go too far, which I did, sooo many times, and still never learnt.

The trouble is, as one of Jeremy's friends who worked in advertising once said, 'One drink is never enough, two is just right, three are never enough.' You'll get to hear, and I'm sure be horrified, or amused, or perhaps both, by many of my and Clarkson's alcohol-fuelled escapades right through this book. But drugs are a no-go for me, for so many reasons. Firstly, I'm terrified of what the totally unregulated, haven't-got-a-clue-what's-in-them party treats will do to me (even alcohol can quite easily have a catastrophic effect on me, with the right disastrous mix). Secondly, they're illegal, and I generally like to stay on the right side of the law, save for the odd speeding error or parking incident. Thirdly, I hate what they actually do to a party; that is, half the participants disappear in a secretive huddle like schoolchildren trying to hide a stink-bomb attack outside the headmaster's office. In fact, the deceit annoys me the most; one, don't take me for a fool, and lying is just rude. And another thing (and then I'll stop ranting), while the users and abusers are off hidden in a loo somewhere, the gently tipsy folk are left wondering why a fun conversation was just cut short and the room/garden is suddenly half empty. It just ruins the jolly flow.

However, I do have to put my hand up at this point and say that I have ruined the jolly flow of a party when I've suddenly been hit by room spin and had to go and have an in-depth chat with the lavatory, and that leads me back to my innate fear of what the hell would drugs do to me!?

So now we've got my view on drugs straight, 'porno man' disappeared to get his hit and I was left with a few quite urbane gentlemen who were fascinated by my *Top Gear* stories and the fact that I could chat football too, which helped me charm one of the guests, a Geordie, who seemed a little out of place, a bit like me. It turned out he used to work in horse racing, which is the world my ex worked in, and they knew each other, so we chatted away about various bods in the racing world and I found myself very relaxed indeed in this extraordinary new world I'd found myself in. I later found out that he was not Jeremy's favourite person, as the gossip was that he was a real social climber and had been hitting on Francie, Jeremy's wife. Ooh, the tangled web he'd woven could be a tricky place to be.

Putting that discomfort aside, on the plus side for me I had earned brownie points with the big man for executing my inaugural night out so well. But that was early doors, before drinks four, five and six saw me lowering the tone after one of the chaps had complimented me on a very simple silver ring I was wearing. I was flattered, but also surprised, as most of the women were dripping in diamonds. I have just thought that maybe he was being facetious. Oh well, I took the compliment and went on to explain that I'd had it for years in memory of a school friend who had been killed, tragically young, so it was very important to me and I never took it off; in fact, I explained further, it had actually made my finger narrower. I then jumped in with drunken wit and asked, does that happen to your penises if you masturbate too much? Luckily, even the most urbane, straight-faced, tie-firmly-tied chaps roared with laughter after my best behaviour had clearly left the building, quite a few drinks beforehand. Better yet, Mr Clarkson proclaimed that he was very proud of me and my quick wit, despite it being a bit filthy.

You are probably getting an idea of just how well Jeremy and I rolled together. However, it was a total roller-coaster of a ride and here comes the downside of this particular evening.

The garden and the house were beginning to move, in my opinion, like a large ship in stormy seas. It was time for me to leave. Jeremy, however, was full steam ahead, enjoying the relief of my acceptance into the periphery of his exclusive circle of friends, leading me slowly to the inner sanctum of the infamous Chipping Norton Set.

As I'm sure many of you who are part of a couple will agree, exiting a party can be a lengthy process. I think you have to agree your strategy at the beginning of the evening. If it's an intimate dinner party, perhaps have a secret code of scratching your left ear or making an announcement of your early start in the morning, which was perfect for Jeremy as he so often had one, with his demanding film schedule, and it could be any day of the week. Plan or no plan, if you start trying to say goodnight to all your favourite acquaintances and find the hosts, who in this particular instance were not on good terms, so if you could find one, you couldn't find the other, you're in trouble. On this occasion, both he and his wife were in and out of arguments, often disappearing with close allies to escape the personal crisis they were in. For some reason, Jeremy was insistent on finding Tom to say goodbye.

We eventually wobbled home to what we fondly called our 'tree-house', Jeremy's penthouse flat, luckily, given the state we were in, just a few hundred yards away. Upon successfully navigating the security system to the building, the lift and the challenging huge front door to the flat, I de-robed quite quickly and headed for bed, leaving Jeremy to draw on one last fag before he called it a night. Or so I thought.

The next thing I recall is waking up with that dreaded woozy feeling, firmly registering you've overdone it and desperately needing a wee, with a fervent hope that my notorious vomiting was not about to commence. As I managed to extricate myself from the bed and battle my way through the over-sized, heavy and annoyingly hidden bedroom doors – a so-called clever design feature – I heard voices upstairs.

After relieving myself in the bathroom, I covered myself up with one of Jeremy's shirts that he'd left strewn on the bathroom floor and mountaineered the stairs to find Tom had left his own party. Completely 'wired', he was chattering away with Jeremy.

I was bemused, confused and slightly embarrassed standing there in front of a relative stranger half-naked. Tom babbled away and suggested he was just leaving, Jeremy said, 'I'll be down in a minute.' (The master suite was downstairs.)

'A minute' went on all night and, as I woke up for the second time, with a classic morning hangover in the cold light of day, Jeremy still hadn't come to bed! I slowly climbed the stairs again to find him puffing away at the dining table with an overflowing ashtray (a common sight). 'What are you doing?' I asked.

'Tom needed a chat,' he replied. 'He's going through a hard time, like me.' (He was referring to his separation from his wife.) He went to bed. I drank a pint of water and joined him. And that was the end of the 'first night'.

* * * *

We had a few more peripheral social-circle dinners and started to go out as a couple for dinner, at places like Heston Blumenthal's Dinner restaurant at the Mandarin Oriental in Knightsbridge. We were well looked after, as you might imagine, and especially as JC had put in a call to Heston himself to get the table. Jeremy always boasted how he could get a table anywhere, and he was not wrong. Partly due to his celebrity status, but also because he wrote for both *The Sun* and *The Times*, and we all know Jeremy's not afraid of speaking out if someone has let him down or upset him. Add to that the fact that one of his closest friends was A A Gill, the late *Sunday Times* restaurant critic, and he certainly never went hungry.

At Heston's we had the best table in the house, overlooking the garden and the park beyond. We were suitably entertained by Heston's magical and extraordinary culinary delights such as foie gras, or pâté of some sort, served up heavily disguised as an orange. It truly was amazing, all edible, but it literally looked like I'd been served an orange with a piece of toast – a little disconcerting as the image of an orange disguising the meaty pâté really messed with your taste buds and your mind. I distinctly remember Jeremy had bone marrow and was literally served a bone, as you would give to your dog; this was also very disconcerting and disturbing, although very apt, I suppose, for a neanderthal oaf like Clarkson. I took a picture of him begging like a dog over it.

Pudding was perhaps Heston's most famous dish, liquid-nitrogen ice cream, which was theatrically made before us on a specially designed trolley with his bespoke liquid-nitrogen ice cream mixer. It was quite a spectacle, and a great performance by the ice cream maker, who talked us through the event, explaining the unimaginably low temperature of -196 degrees C, which can cause catastrophic burns and has tragically blown a chef's hand off in the past. Thankfully, everything was under control on this occasion as we watched the mystical liquid nitrogen cloud that swirled around as if a magical potion was being mixed.

Talking of nice restaurants, the next big intro was to be to one of Jeremy's closest friends, Adrian Gill, or A A Gill as he was known as *The Sunday Times* food and TV critic. Adrian was known for his brutal and acerbic write-ups and he and Jeremy were kindred spirits. Adrian was also not afraid to speak his mind to anyone, or not to speak to them at all if he didn't like them.

Jeremy was very anxious about introducing me to him and to his long-term girlfriend and girl about town, Nicola Formby, also a very strong character. Nicola was a former model, once photographed by David Bailey for a magazine cover, which helped launch her successful career in modelling. She once played the part of Diana, Princess of Wales, in a Canadian production, *The Women of Windsor*. I've only just found that out whilst I was fact-checking. I also played the part of Princess Di for a photoshoot years ago. People said we were alike – we obviously are.

I wish I had known that on this evening, as it would have helped with my nerves. Jeremy had told me that she could be aloof, and a little intimidating. She was by then a successful food consultant for several London restaurants and she was also involved with the PR of Bicester Village designer outlet.

Jeremy's concerns made me slightly nervous as we headed out to yet another restaurant with long waiting lists for tables, but not when the likes of A A Gill, Nicola Formby, Jeremy Clarkson and Jemima Khan are attending. However, I am generally not fazed by anyone and have been reasonably well brought up to have good manners. But mostly in my favour, as JC went on to compliment me for, I have the ability to read a room and tend to hold myself back before I let the true 'me' come out. I've learned to ask questions about who I'm talking to and listen to their stories before imposing mine, but of course everyone was interested in me, as the big man's new squeeze, and that was a little unnerving. I felt all eyes on me and was sitting right opposite the king of dining, Adrian. I then did become flustered about what to choose from the menu and thought it appropriate to ask the master himself.

Big mistake! Adrian ordered some salt-crusted fish (I'm sure there was a much more glamorous and appealing name for it, but I can't remember). It arrived with a huge actual crust of salt on it, which I really wasn't sure what to do with, and then, of course, it had millions of bones to deal with, which I absolutely hate. Dear Adrian was actually a sensitive, kind soul despite his reputation; he saw my fear and dismay reassuringly quickly and ordered the kitchen to de-crust and debone my fish immediately.

Adrian and I then went on, led by him, to take the piss out of Jeremy all evening. One of his first questions being, 'Why? Why would someone as lovely as you choose to be with someone as awful as him?' Adrian's departing comment to Jeremy regarding me, as we said goodbye, was, 'Great tits!' Some of you may be appalled by that, but I thought it was hilarious and a great affirmation of my acceptance into the fold. I was doubly relieved when both Nicola Formby and Jemima Khan gave their seal of approval too.

* * * *

From then on, our social life accelerated at a speed I struggled to keep up with, whilst I was also touring the world with *Top Gear Live* and being a single mum. I was stretched, but Jeremy was juggling filming and writing for BBC *Top Gear*, both in locations all over the world and in the studio whilst the series was being screened, as well as writing three newspaper columns and for *Top Gear Magazine*. He was also moving between his family home in Oxfordshire (whilst negotiating a separation from his wife), my house in Hertfordshire and the flat in London. No wonder he went off the rails.

For as long as I have known Jeremy, which is over twenty years, he has spent half of his week, if not filming in some exotic location, based in London. Whilst in town he would be out pretty much every single night – at film previews, bar openings, restaurants, friends' birthdays, dinners or parties. In the early days we would have nights in to avoid being seen and would enjoy a take-away or cook for each other and watch a movie. Once I had been accepted, I was included in the unending invitations.

Jeremy is incredibly well connected and, as he became more and more famous, many acquaintances would value his presence at their film premières, preview screenings and openings. He is one of the original influencers. He also had to fit in screenings of films in which his *Top Gear* guests were starring, to do research for his interviews. The few I went to were put on for Jeremy exclusively and we would sit in a private screening room enjoying the latest blockbuster. The only downside was that there was no atmosphere, no tasty snacks, no feeling of suspense or excitement from fellow viewers.

Jeremy's other homework for *Top Gear* would be occasionally to entertain the celebrity guest. To be honest, if he wasn't personally interested in them, he would have got out of it, but on the occasion when I had the pleasure of joining in, it was with one of his screen heroes, Kiefer Sutherland, best known for his role as Jack Bauer in the hugely successful series *24*.

Jeremy messaged me at the last minute, a common occurrence, and said, how did I fancy joining him and a Hollywood star for dinner. I was not a fan of *24* so didn't really know anything about Kiefer except that he was a child actor in one of my favourite teen movies *The Lost Boys*.

We met Kiefer at his hotel, a five-star, very grand hotel on Regent Street in London. We went through to the bar and a member of staff put a call through to Kiefer's room. When he eventually arrived I was so shocked at how small he was; not only short, but a slight man too. Not dissimilar to Richard Hammond. Like Richard, he was very attractive and had that celebrity presence.

He very quickly ordered a double scotch and then we all ordered a light supper. Kiefer was not a big eater, but was definitely a BIG drinker. He was charming, funny and had some great anecdotes, but I'm afraid I can't remember any of them. You'll understand why by the end of this, my own little anecdote.

I bonded with Kiefer quite quickly as he is a massive horse-lover and once gave up on his career as an actor to take up professional rodeo. He still owned a lot of horses and his current on-off partner was a keen horsewoman too. Jeremy rolled his eyes and moaned about us nattering on about horses. It was one of those evenings that organically (not very organic) morphed into an epic night out. Despite Kiefer saying that he ought to go to bed as he had an early flight, he joined us outside on the steps of the hotel entrance and had a fag with Jezza. It was then spontaneously decided to go to Jeremy's private members' club in Mayfair. A cab was hailed and we soon arrived at the prestigious venue. We went through to the internal courtyard where all the smokers could hang out.

As soon as we were approached by a waiter, Kiefer said, 'I'll have a triple scotch, it will save you time.' Oh dear, this was clearly going to get messy. And it did. When Kiefer started picking the plants that were for decoration and presenting them to me as a gift and I was stroking his arm, enquiring what all his tattoos meant, Jeremy decided it was time to leave.

Jeremy and I jumped in a cab, but Kiefer said he'd walk, which, to be honest, he was really struggling to do, so I said to Jeremy that we should get him safely back to his hotel. The big man was past caring, so off we went, leaving Kiefer bouncing off the kerbs around the streets of Mayfair.

Jeremy got a message from him the next day. He had missed his flight. rock 'n' roll! And he is a true rock-'n'-roller: not only is he an accomplished actor, who was engaged briefly to Julia Roberts, he also released a first album in 2016 called *Not Enough Whiskey*. I know where he got that idea from!

*   *   *   *

Jeremy loved film and TV; we got hooked on *Breaking Bad* and *Game of Thrones*. Both these series were actually a blessing for me, helping me to keep the big man still and relaxed for a while. It was also part of his job to stay abreast of popular culture and these epics were a good source of inspiration for ideas for *Top Gear* content.

He belonged to an exclusive film club run by Nicola Formby and Eric Fellner, CEO of Working Title Films, which has made classics like *Four Weddings and a Funeral*, the Bridget Jones films, *Love Actually*, the Mr Bean movies, *Nanny McPhee*, *Rush* and *The Theory of Everything*, to name just a few. Eric's main office in the heart of London has a cool, and very comfortable, private cinema, to which Nicola arranged visits by many notable characters: journalist Christa D'Souza; theatre impresario Nick Allott (Cameron Mackintosh's main man); film producer Nick Love; journalist Alice B-B (full name Alice Brudenell-Bruce); actor Johnny Standing and his wife Sarah, the sister of TV's Emma Forbes and daughter of Nanette Newman, who was a sixties and seventies film icon and the face and hands of a long-running Fairy Liquid ad campaign. Jemima Khan was also a regular – less well known is that she is a film producer herself – also Henrietta Conrad, who works with Jemima, A A Gill and, my favourite, Hugh Grant. It was rather special to watch films with the people who were in them.

We went to many screenings, some just for fun, of old, classic movies and others about to be launched, being run past all these worldly characters for their critiques and support. Jemima Khan had produced a documentary on the Wikileaks saga. It was a full house in the mini-cinema, and we'd all settled in. The film had been running for a few minutes when a latecomer snuck in, carrying a scooter helmet, and tried discreetly to make his way to his seat.

It was Hugh Grant! I struggled to remain calm and pretend to Jeremy that the fact that my one-and-only screen heartthrob had just walked in was not exciting at all. After the screening, I rushed to the loo, and as I left the corridor leading to the unisex facilities, I opened the door and bumped straight into Hugh with his helmet (no innuendos, please). Trying desperately to remain cool, I apologised for bumping into him, at which point he came out with the best line I've ever heard, 'Well, hellohh!' Sooo Hugh Grant. He is totally Daniel Cleaver (the womaniser from the Bridget Jones movies). He was even dressed in exactly the same way: open shirt, beige chinos, classic suede shoes. I will take that moment to my grave. Little did I know there would be a far better sequel …

Weirdly, and I'm sure some of you will find this very hard to believe, but Jeremy reminded me of Hugh. They are both womanisers in real life, devoted to schoolboy humour and still showing no signs of growing up. But, a bit like Mr Darcy and Daniel Cleaver, they don't care too much for each other. Too similar, I suspect.

3

The Best Hotel in the World

Having been approved by Jemima Khan, I was regularly kindly invited to her wonderful house in the country for the weekend. These treat weekends were a bit of an antidote to the wild parties and relentlessly fast-paced life which Jeremy and I were living at this time. We were both touring with *Top Gear Live* all over the world and I was also working on other events, including Carfest, with Chris Evans, and managing home life with my son, who has special needs. Jeremy was writing his columns, writing and recording the studio scenes for *Top Gear* and travelling far and wide, filming the usual car reviews plus the epic specials that we all know and love – and these could take up to two weeks to film. He was also managing to appear on *QI*, *Have I Got News for You* and the like. His schedule was ridiculous, and relentless. So, an invitation to Jemima's luxury retreat was always very welcome.

Jemima became a good ally and we spent numerous weekends at what Jeremy and I called 'the best hotel in the world'. If you don't know of Jemima, she is the daughter of the late James Goldsmith, a financier, tycoon and politician. Jemima, along with her siblings, is the heiress to his fortune.

Her mother was formerly married to Mark Birley, who opened the famous nightclub Annabel's, which was named after her. It is reportedly the only nightclub that the Queen has ever been to.

Annabel's was set up in the early sixties in the basement of John Aspinall's casino. John, a friend of Birley, wanted somewhere to hang out into the wee small hours after a night's gambling. By all accounts, it was the place to be in the swinging sixties. Apart from the Queen, some of the other big stars who have hung out there or performed are: Karen Carpenter; Olivia Newton-John; Tina Turner; Diana Ross; Ray Charles; and, more recently, Lady Gaga. It certainly was, and still is, the place to be, if you belong to this incredible social circle.

Jemima's mother, Annabel, went on to marry James Goldsmith and have two more children: Ben, a financier and environmentalist, who was married first to Kate Rothschild, another heiress to one of Britain's most powerful banking dynasties; and Zac, currently a Member of the House of Lords.

Jemima herself was married to ex-Pakistan cricketer Imran Khan, who went on to become Pakistan's prime minister. Confused? I was, most of the time, with everyone's titles and family histories. I think if I'd known all their titles and histories, I would have been very daunted, but as it was, I just took everyone at face value. But I'm sure you're getting a sense now that Jeremy does not hang out with James May and Richard Hammond, having a pint down the pub and tinkering with cars, when not working.

Jemima was so warm and welcoming and created a wonderful relaxed and friendly atmosphere, whether it was at her incredibly cool and private mews house in West London, which Jeremy was actually considering buying (it was reportedly on sale for a price in excess of £7 million!), or on her country estate in the Cotswolds, Kiddington, which comprises a manor house and converted stables providing at least eight bedroom suites, several self-contained cottages, separate houses, a cinema, a gym, an orangery/bar/pool/party room, swimming pool, paddocks, stables, a tennis court and a lake. Jemima bought it in a terrible state and went about giving it an incredible makeover, from which we benefited greatly. I cannot remember how many weekends we spent there, but it became our weekend retreat, and was simply wonderful.

Jemima is incredibly kind and generous and invited along with us some of her family members, mutual friends, Nicola and Adrian Gill and their children, many of the others who were part of the film club and a fantastic array of fascinating characters such as the designer Bella Freud, daughter of the artist Lucian Freud, himself the grandson of Sigmund Freud, the notorious psychoanalyst, and somewhere along the line related to Matthew Freud, who will pop up later in my story. Bella's husband is James Fox, an American journalist and author of *White Mischief*, which was made into a film starring Charles Dance and Greta Scacchi. He also co-wrote the bestselling memoir of The Rolling Stones guitarist, Keith Richards.

My recollection of Bella and James is that they were both gentle and kind souls, who had a lovely dog, which was never far from wherever we were eating. I was such a no one amongst all these amazing people, but somehow, I managed to fit in. Another big name who appeared one weekend was Michael Gambon and his mistress, interior designer Philippa Hart. Philippa and I became kindred spirits as she was also a mistress, if slightly more involved with her man than me. Michael put her up in a flat in London with their two boys whilst he remained married to his wife and spent half his time in the family home elsewhere.

I first met another of my TV heroes, Richard Bacon and his long-suffering wife Rebecca, at a classic weekend at Jemima's.

Richard and Jeremy were party partners in crime and Rebecca and I did a lot of eye-rolling at their discussions and behaviour, but they were both incredibly quick-witted and very funny together.

There were also more intellectual types, including none other than the great philosopher and author Alain de Botton. When I sat next to him at lunch one weekend, I had no idea who he was. It's only since I've left that world that I've realised. I'd just known him as Alain. I wish I'd known then; I have so enjoyed and admired his books and podcasts. I would have gone so much further with our discussion about what love is, but at the time I felt protective about my personal life, obviously, as it was with one of the most famous people on the planet.

Another notable guest was Tom Hollander, most famous at the time for his role as Adam Smallbone in the BBC sitcom *Rev*, in which he played alongside Olivia Colman. He wrote it, too. Tom, who dated Jemima for a while, is a very talented man who has gone on to play some really strong and sinister characters such as Major Lance 'Corky' Corkoran in the spy thriller *The Night Manager*. He was such good fun, and so grounded. I had the pleasure of sitting next to him over a whole weekend; we were like naughty schoolchildren at one end of the dining table.

Arriving at Jemima's was heaven. You'd be welcomed by her loyal and very accommodating staff and her beautiful white, long-haired Alsatian, Brian. The housekeepers would show you to your suite for the weekend. We were often given the Red Room, which really was quite red and would have fitted quite well into a scene in the film *Fifty Shades of Grey*. It had a four-poster bed and a beautiful double shower area, rather than a cubicle, tiled with a Moroccan-style mosaic. Just as in a hotel, you could ring down to the staff quarters and request anything you needed.

We would often arrive to join all the other guests for lunch, served outside in summer by the pool on a table decorated with flowers from the garden. The pool was a unique round one just off the huge orangery, which had changing rooms and a shower alongside, a bar and several sumptuous lounging areas perfect for afternoon snoozes if it wasn't warm enough to lie by the pool.

Jemima created an incredibly relaxed vibe and offered pretty much anything you could wish for: Polaris Quad safaris, tennis, boating on the lake, zip-wiring across the lake, walking around the extensive grounds, riding, tennis, massage – anything you wanted could be provided. Jeremy mainly read, ate, drank and snoozed. I loved to be able to say, 'I'm just off for a ride,' which I'm lucky enough to be able to do in my own life at home. At Jemima's, though, you asked one of the staff to put a call in to the groom, and you were then notified when your horse was ready. Being a DIY horse person, I liked to go to the yard early and groom and, more importantly for me, meet the horse which Hugh Grant had bought Jemima. (I could dream. Jeremy did once threaten to buy me a horse with the help of his good friend Charlie Brooks, who, as an ex-jockey, apparently knew everyone there was to know in the horse world, and was sure to be able to find one suitable for me. It never happened.)

Once the horse had been groomed and tacked up, I was then free to set off over the hills and far away with the backdrop of the majestic Grade ll-listed manor house and Capability Brown-designed gardens. It felt like living in a movie. When the season came, there would be shooting parties. Not my favourite pastime, apart from the fresh winter air and warming food and drink.

It was wonderful. Everyone was free to do exactly as they pleased, and all reconvened for a delicious and entertaining supper at which there was never a dull moment. However, these were really tame compared to Jeremy's other friends' suppers and all were usually in bed by midnight at the latest. Jemima's not a big drinker and so many of the guests were recovering alcoholics and/or drug addicts. By contrast, most of the others were still on it, but opted for a quiet time in these idyllic surroundings, unless of course it was a party night.

Breakfast was served in the huge kitchen and was available when you were ready, with an extensive menu on offer like any good country hotel. Most assembled around nine and would enjoy a slow start to another idyllic day in the Cotswolds. All the Sunday newspapers would be laid out. Most of the guests were in these, having either written a piece, or having been written about. It was quite bizarre, and fascinating, to listen to the other side of stories which were so often embellished, or nowhere near the truth.

After a walk or whatever activity took your fancy, a wonderful roast dinner would be served in the dining room, which was very comfortable, not ostentatious, as you might imagine. Nor was any part of the house, really. It was very tastefully put together: cosy and welcoming, despite the overall size of the house. The only thing that I wasn't sure about was the stuffed giraffe which stood in the hall, reaching up to the top of the stairwell. I love giraffes, but I wasn't too keen to see a lifeless one as a rather over-the-top ornament. Although there is an argument that it had died, or at worst was killed, and is at least now being honoured for the rest of time as the majestic creature that it was.

Talking of tasteful, that was not what Michael Gambon thought of the newly completed drawing room. He famously, and a little controversially amongst all the regular guests, was incredibly outspoken and basically declared it a mess.

He was very funny, Sir Michael, basically a Londoner done good (even though he was actually born in Dublin but came to London with his family when he was young), who by his own account had struck it lucky doing what he loved and had seemingly winged his way through an extraordinary life. He told us in his most natural default East End accent the incredible story of how he made up his CV to follow his passion for acting and to get out of his factory apprenticeship.

He landed up being spotted by Laurence Olivier, who recognised his natural talent. Of course, most of us now know him as Professor Dumbledore. However, despite his amusing tales and anecdotes, I don't think after sharing his personal view on Jemima's design decisions he was invited back for a fabulous sleepover at Ms Goldsmith's manor.

The reluctant endings to these idyllic weekends were afternoon tea served whilst we were all snuggled up in the TV room watching the Grand Prix or another sporting event or out in the quintessentially English country garden. Then it was time for goodbyes, tipping the staff and, more often than not, for Jeremy and me to go our separate ways.

4

Weeknights

The weekends at Jemima's were a great way for me to get to know Jeremy's closest allies, none more so than Adrian Gill and Nicola Formby. They were the king and queen of restaurant life and the general social scene in London, and beyond. Nicola is a fantastic facilitator and networker. We got on very well, I think, because we both had tricky partners to manage and our children were of a similar age. Jeremy loved it that this high-society couple had embraced little old me and we often had dinner, just the four of us, and, eventually, we went on to holiday together.

For the time being, it was dinners at some of the best restaurants and with the best company. One of Jeremy's favourites was The Wolseley, where we were once invited to the private dining room to celebrate the founder and CEO Jeremy King's birthday, or was it just another day in a West End restaurant manager's life? My memory fails me on the detail, but it was all very special and exciting as we were led through the main dining area past the likes of past and present James Bonds, pop stars and numerous TV personalities, lords and ladies interspersed with the odd Joe Public, who had no doubt saved for months for their special treat of a dinner.

We passed them all with a slight sense of superiority, to climb a staircase which led to a secret dining room where we joined more of the elite of this extraordinary social circle of which Jeremy was a highly regarded member. A far cry from having a roadside burger with James May and Richard Hammond on one of their infamous road trips.

We had intimate dinners with so many celebs, such as Liz Hurley, one of the original supermodels of the eighties and one of Hugh Grant's old flames, and lovely Dougray Scott, who has the best 'claim to fame' story, having been chosen by Tom Cruise to play the villain in *Mission Impossible 2*. He's also been Superman's ex Terri Hatcher's love interest in *Desperate Housewives*. He was with his real love interest at most of the dinners we had with him, Claire Forlani, who has starred alongside legends such as Sean Connery in *The Rock* and Anthony Hopkins and Brad Pitt in *Meet Joe Black*.

These dinners were my favourite thing. Although at first it felt a little surreal being amongst all the Hollywood stars, I really enjoyed the company of all these creative and fascinating types, who, at the end of the day, were just people with extraordinary jobs. When we dined with just a few, Jeremy was relaxed and we all just shared the trials and tribulations of normal life juggled between international travel, demanding schedules and complicated family life.

The real showstopper nights in the city that never sleeps, even on a school night, were at Mr and Mrs Jimmy Carr's. My first introduction to Jimmy and his partner Caroline (they are not actually married) was at a dinner party at their showstopper house in Primrose Hill in a road the equal of the Hollywood Hills, where each house is a pristine mansion, interior-designed from top to bottom, a place where a tour to spot celebrities could be a sell-out.

After making it through the security gates, the massive solid front door slowly opened and we were greeted by uniformed staff who took our coats in what looked like a hotel foyer, albeit a minimalistic one. It was hard to see where the doors were amongst the pristine lines of wood and marble that dressed the floor and walls. Jeremy couldn't wait to see if I could make my way to the loo and find how to get back again. I did manage, but it was daunting as you had to find the button or sensor to open the automatic sliding door of the loo and pray that it wouldn't suddenly open whilst you were pulling your drawers up!

After being served canapés and champagne, we were led through to the vast dining room where I was seated next to David Walliams and his then wife, model Lara Stone, and opposite David Mitchell and his girlfriend Victoria Coren. Jimmy and Caroline were so welcoming and I felt very lucky to be accepted into this world of high achievers. Keep reading to find out more about what I called Jimmy Carr's 'celebtastic' parties, which were held on a monthly basis at least.

My next big introduction to Jeremy's inner circle of friends was at his private members' club, 5 Hertford Street, Mayfair, run by Jemima Khan's half-brother, Robin, where I met her brother Ben Goldsmith. The club, where we'd enjoyed our drunken evening with Kiefer Sutherland, is reputed to be the most secret in London.

Jeremy had arranged to meet Dom, a really close friend from his Chipping Norton inner sanctum. There would be just the three of us. Sadly, Dom's wife had recently died. They had formerly all hung out as a foursome, with Jeremy's wife, Francie. This was a daunting evening, especially in such a prestigious setting which felt like it belonged only to the great and the good, let alone the fact that I was 'the other woman' meeting one of the Clarkson family's closest friends.

Outside, the men providing security at the door recognised Jeremy immediately, of course, although he had only recently become a member. Actually, I got the feeling he would have been let in anyway, member or not. I, however, needed to be signed in officially, but, once through the second layer of security, I was welcomed into what was essentially a Mayfair townhouse which provides sumptuous, intimate dining areas and has a beautiful courtyard for smokers, which, of course, is where we headed first.

Dom arrived and we headed to our table, passing Dame Joan Collins on the way. Once again, I passed the test of acceptance and the evening rolled on, continuing back in the courtyard where I met more close friends, Belle and John Robinson. John founded the fashion retailer Jigsaw, which famously employed Catherine Middleton (prior to her marriage to Prince William). John was very welcoming and I loved hearing how he had started in the business, travelling to Europe to buy up hippy Afghan coats, with which he filled his car to bring back to sell on market stalls. Belle and I also hit it off and she became a good friend to me. She was also very close to Jeremy and they often had blow-out all-nighters together, especially when, sadly, her marriage broke down.

This evening had another messy ending, with us dancing away in the basement club of the very exclusive millionaire playground, safe from prying eyes. It wasn't my favourite place. There was something sinister about it, too. I suspect the precious privacy the club offered was to protect the not so great and the not too good, too.

* * * *

Weeknights were packed for Mr Clarkson, with never a dull moment, especially after he was thrown out of the family home and was residing mainly in the flat in Holland Park. If he wasn't working, he was out. He had a never-ending stream of invitations to film premières, dinners, fundraisers, launches and openings of this, that and the other.

Once we were in a taxi on the way to an event at The Ivy, the original one in the West End, and he admitted he didn't know who'd invited him and what it was in aid of. As it turned out, there were a number of people he knew there and we eventually sat down for another delicious dinner accompanied by Jemima Khan, Alice B-B, Jimmy Carr and Uma Thurman. Jeremy loved to boast about Uma once sitting on his knee whilst they were away skiing some years before. He couldn't take his eyes off her, especially when she climbed over our fellow diners in order to 'powder her nose', revealing what so many men can only dream of.

I was fascinated by this extraordinary 'social club' which I had accidently become part of. It actually had quite a small membership and, as Jeremy would say, 'all the usual suspects' would roll out for the next restaurant opening or film preview. A lot of these events are well documented in the endless tabloid reports seared online for ever, as we got 'papped' time and time again.

The made-up headlines made me laugh every time. A classic example was when we left a huge celebratory dinner, David Tang's sixtieth at The Dorchester on Park Lane, and it was reported that we had left separately. Jeremy had supposedly left with another blonde, Boris Johnson's sister, Rachel Johnson. The truth was that I was just a few feet ahead of Jeremy and Rachel, with Rachel's husband. Another night we were with Rachel and the newspaper she actually wrote for reported on her being 'just another blonde', whom it appeared they couldn't identify!

That night was particularly mind-blowing. I had never heard of Sir David Tang until then. It was at his 'intimate' sixtieth celebrations with over 500 guests, who were without exception titled, millionaires or billionaires or well-known celebrities, or all three! Except me!

Sir David is possibly the most intriguing character of all those I met in my whirlwind relationship with Jeremy. David Tang began life in Hong Kong and, by all accounts, went from rags to riches to rags again. He was clearly a very clever man, weaving his way (literally − he was big in the fashion retail industry) into the lives and businesses of very powerful and influential people. He became an advisor to huge brands such as the Savoy Hotel Group, Tommy Hilfiger and the high-end jewellers Asprey & Garrard. He was, bizarrely, the Agony Uncle for the *Financial Times* and wrote about his night in the Kremlin with President Putin. Amongst his vast and eclectic friendship group were Fidel Castro, the Duke of Malborough, Princess Diana, Margaret Thatcher, the Queen (whose Balmoral shooting parties he used to get invited to), and Tracey Emin. He loved the arts, cigars, ballet and dressing flamboyantly − he was often seen in velvet suits and silk cravats. He was also a great philanthropist and made good use of all his wealthy and high-profile friends. I could write reams about him, but there are already a number of fascinating books out there, both written by him and about him.

Back to Sir David's lavish birthday celebration: it was as if I'd landed in Madame Tussauds and all the waxworks had come to life to be joined by a pop-up version of *Hello* and *Tatler* magazines. I came face to bosom with Eva Herzigová, of Wonderbra fame, was blown away rubbing shoulders with Sir Michael Caine, was dwarfed by Miss Naomi Campbell hanging out with her old buddy Kate Moss, felt desperately sorry for Miss Tara Palmer-Tomkinson, who was clearly so vulnerable that she even latched onto me for security. It truly was like being in a mad dream.

Having arrived at this packed and vibrant party, I soon lost Jeremy in the champagne-fuelled throng. Luckily, the incredibly caring and most genuine of men, Shaun Woodward, rescued me from my slight panic attack, set off by being no one and knowing no one.

Shaun was perhaps the kindest man I met during my incredible time in Clarkson's mad world and we kept in touch even after my split from Jeremy. He is the former husband of Camilla Sainsbury, the supermarket heiress, and another very kind person. He was the Secretary of State for Northern Ireland under Gordon Brown's premiership and the Under Secretary of State for Creative Industries and Tourism when Tony Blair was prime minister.

Before becoming an MP, Shaun had worked in television with the likes of Esther Rantzen and was a director of her charity Childline. He famously defected from the Conservatives to join the Labour Party after major disagreements on gay rights. He has since come out as gay. With all that eclectic experience and personal trauma, he comes across as a wonderfully rounded, wise and caring person, and was a great support to Jeremy when things blew up over 'that punch'. More about the Sainsburys later. I wish there were more people like Shaun in our current government, and in life generally.

Back to that party. After downing a few glasses of champagne, I eventually found my big man again. I couldn't lose him for long with that crazy hair and all six-foot-five-inches of him. We made our way to our table, picking our way past the Duchess of York, Sir Tom Jones, Sir Philip Green, Sir Stuart Rose, CEO of M&S at the time, and the Candy brothers, entrepreneurs like our host, but probably the youngest there, mere babes of property tycoonship. I began to wonder who on earth I was going to be seated next to.

Lucky me. After circling our table, reading place names, Jeremy assured me I would be well looked after by the most amusing and welcoming Viscount Linley, son of Princess Margaret, nephew of our great queen. Also known as the 2nd

Earl of Snowdon, David Albert Charles Armstrong-Jones, or 'the carpenter', as Jeremy liked to call him, because he's known for his furniture-making business.

David, as he is known to his friends, made me feel very welcome and, to my surprise, we had a great laugh together with the other lords and ladies on our table, including his long-suffering wife, Serena. It's hard being the partner of a party animal, as I was beginning to become aware.

Weirdly, I can't remember much about the entertainment. The guest list was enough for me. I was constantly distracted by people-watching, no ordinary people-watching. I know there was an orchestra playing at some point, which was pretty impressive, if not really my cup of tea.

Well, all good things come to an end and this epic party was no exception. We were amongst the hard-core party-goers, continuing to mingle with the star-studded crowd and among the last to leave. Sir David actually had a reputation for calling time at his social gatherings; he was reported to end an evening with, 'Thank you all for coming, now f**k off home.'

As we made our way out past the die-hard partygoers, I absolutely loved (excuse the pun, but I genuinely did) meeting Joanna Lumley, who was everything you would imagine her to be, charming, funny, but, above all, genuine. She remains someone whom I wholly admire and look up to, even though, in actual fact, I physically looked down on her. She was much shorter than I expected, but absolutely gorgeous, both inside and out. In true 'Patsy' style, she too was among the last to leave, spellbound by who and what we had just experienced.

The most disappointing person I met was, thankfully, as we were leaving. I had no interest in meeting him at all, but found myself in an awkward unwanted (by me) handshake with Tony Blair. He was also forced to look up to all six-foot-plus of me. He is small and as smarmy as he looks in pictures. He clearly loved being at such an event and was keen to be the centre of attention, but was easily lost in the crowd, especially the crowd that David Tang had brought together.

* * * *

Not long after this event, Sir David invited Jeremy to do a Q and A at one of his charitable projects, the China Exchange in Chinatown. Not a fan of this type of evening, JC reluctantly donned one of his few suits with the aim of looking grown up and being taken seriously. We headed in to the West End to find the old telephone exchange which David had bought and transformed into a venue to support the Chinese community – a place where anyone can learn about China, Chinese culture and history and London's Chinatown. Its aim is to strengthen the relationship between the UK and China.

Jeremy was unusually anxious, something I'd witnessed on only a few occasions, but if he's put in a situation where he's not in control, he can get surprisingly nervous. His biggest fear was that there would be a journalist there trying to catch him out over one of his controversial moments. He had nothing to worry about as David facilitated the evening and gave him an intro that he himself said was not really required. Jeremy then fielded the questions and all was well. David then insisted he take us to dinner at his famous China Tang restaurant in the Dorchester Hotel.

And the only way to get there, of course, was in a Roller. Sir David insisted we join him in his chauffeur-driven Rolls-Royce (or Bentley – I can't be clear as we were bundled in at speed as we were being hounded by paparazzi). Now that's the way to arrive at a Park Lane hotel.

We were led through to a private dining area and joined by some lords and ladies, more friends of David, and yet again we were treated like royalty. There was one ugly moment when Sir David blew his top at a member of staff for folding a napkin in the wrong way, or something equally trivial.

I've since learned that he was renowned for losing his temper and for being a real tyrant as well as a jolly socialite whom so many had adored to be around. Sadly, on his early death at the age of sixty-three, the ugly truth was revealed, perhaps explaining why he was so short-tempered. He was holding together a totally fabricated empire, the assets of which he had mainly gambled away. It's reported that he once gave a croupier a £90,000 tip!! His widow was left with nothing other than the extravagant gifts which had been given to him by people in high places, including royalty. She was forced to auction all she had left at Sotheby's, somewhere Sir David would once have been seen in his alter ego as a successful and very wealthy art aficionado and collector.

* * * *

The Last Supper: I don't mean mine and Jeremy's, but the final introduction to Jeremy's inner circle of friends and allies, when I probably felt most daunted. And what a backdrop it was for the meeting with Rebekah and Charlie Brooks. Potentially, it was going to be their last supper with their close friends Sir Charles and Lady Celia Dunstone, who hosted the evening, serving up good old-fashioned comfort food, cottage pie, Charlie's favourite, and something to be savoured when one is facing the prospect of prison in the foreseeable future. Both Rebekah and Charlie were facing serious charges in the *News of the World* phone-hacking trial.

I had actually worked for Sir Charles before, running a promotion for Carphone Warehouse, which he founded with David Ross, who I dated briefly (big mistake!). The theory of six degrees of separation kept cropping up while I was being woven into Jeremy's exclusive social circle, so, although I often felt like a real outsider, I actually had my own connections with quite a few of the people in Jeremy's world, too.

However, I'd never dreamt that I'd be heading to the Dunstones' house to meet arguably the most controversial couple of the moment in the house of a billionaire whose neighbours were Gary Barlow and Simon Cowell. You couldn't make it up!

Jeremy had talked a lot about Rebekah and Charlie; he was very close to them. They were neighbours in Chipping Norton, Oxfordshire, where Jeremy's family home is. Jeremy's children were bridesmaids at Rebekah and Charlie's wedding and he was a godfather, I think, to the Brooks's daughter. In any event, they were very close and, of course, Jeremy effectively worked for Rebekah as she was CEO of News International, which runs *The Sun* and *The Sunday Times* – until, that is, she was caught up in the phone-hacking scandal and was forced to resign.

Jeremy often boasted about how he had instigated their relationship at a dinner party at his house whilst Jeremy was still with his wife. Rebekah had previously been married to Ross Kemp, of *EastEnders* fame.

Jeremy had remained friends with Ross, often having dinner with him, no doubt discussing Ross's latest daredevil documentary, following street gangs, pirates or soldiers on the front line. Ross and Jeremy were also linked via the Help for Heroes charity and *The Sun*'s Military Awards, which has an annual ceremony. Jeremy and Ross would be summoned by Prince Charles to decide which members of the British armed forces would be honoured each year.

So, getting back to the extraordinary kitchen supper at Sir Charles and Lady Dunstone's, I was terrified of getting tongue-tied. Jeremy had told me of how clever and well-read Rebekah was and, of course, both I and the world at large knew just how well-connected she was, as the stories kept coming from one of the biggest courtroom dramas we'd ever known. She was famously linked to the then prime minister David Cameron, former school chum of Charlie and their Chipping Norton neighbour. At the time, there was a great hoo-ha about them all riding out together with Mr Cameron mounted on an ex-police horse, suggesting inappropriate relationships between the media, the government and the police.

There was also the much-reported guest list for their wedding. It was mind-blowing, with arguably the most powerful media mogul in the world, Rupert Murdoch, Rebekah's employer and father figure, topping the leader board for the most influential person there. Also there were the leaders of both the main, political parties, David Cameron and Gordon Brown, keen to gain Mr Murdoch's favour, with Piers Morgan sitting alongside to stir it all up. This extraordinary cast were assembled in the fairy-tale location of Tony Gallagher's (now Sir Tony's, thanks to Boris Johnson) Cotswolds manor house with private chapel.

However, back in the kitchen of the Dunstones' house, Jeremy and I had arrived first. Jeremy hates being late. It is what we argued about most, because I was always late. In my defence, I was usually leaving my boy with a carer, who would need a lengthy handover as a result of all his special needs. I then had to drive thirty-odd miles in to London. But the big man had no patience for my complicated logisitics. Charles and Celia were really welcoming and, thankfully, the focus wasn't on me. Everyone was really concerned about the well-being of Charlie and Rebekah.

Charlie and Rebekah soon arrived and, to my amazement, very early on in the proceedings, Rebekah admitted that she had been very nervous about meeting me. She was clearly fragile, having been fighting for her freedom and for a future with her baby daughter, who was only about two years old at the time. She felt I would judge her for what she was being accused of and was associated with. I was really quite naive at the time and had taken the glowing reference from Jeremy as the truth: that she and Charlie had been caught up in something which they were not responsible for.

I just saw a terrified and worn-out mother, who was clearly very much in love with her husband, and was afraid of losing it all.

There was a lot of talk about politics, which I wasn't really able to keep up with, but other than that, the banter was kept light and, once again, I just felt relieved that I had been accepted and approved of by Mr Clarkson's nearest and dearest.

5

The Golden Triangle

All set for Chipping Norton. Jeremy, as you all now know, has a farm in the Cotswolds. He always claimed he'd bought it for us, though that was after he'd claimed he'd bought it because he needed something to do when we were on one of our breaks. The truth, I later found out, was that he and his wife Francie had bought it as a back-up house in case the proposed rubbish dump went ahead at the back of his beloved family home. The farmland, all 1,000 acres of it, was conveniently just a stone's throw from his existing home, but the farmhouse was far enough away from most things that it would be a great place to escape to, even though it has a public footpath running a few yards from the front door. You can't have everything.

Jeremy and I were at Jemima's one weekend when he took me for the first time to see where our proposed future home was. I'd seen the brochure and was spellbound by the outstanding views. My favourite was through a natural archway of trees that drew you in to the magic of the place, and the extensive views beyond the garden's dry-stone wall over the rolling Cotswold countryside beyond. Having said all that, in reality, the property was really run down. It hadn't been lived in for years and reminded me of Bleak House (from the eponymous book by Charles Dickens), set on top of a hill, one of the highest and coldest points in Oxfordshire, Chadlington, OX6 … Ooh no, I'd better not.

I did actually love the original house and would have liked to have given it an overhaul to turn it into a comfortable family home, but Jeremy had much bigger plans, which, while I grew to love them, I always had concerns about being alone in an enormous house atop a freezing wasteland, whilst Jeremy was off gallivanting around the world.

We loved spending time there, plotting and planning how things would be laid out, where I could keep my beloved horses and other furry and feathered friends, and where Jeremy could grow vegetables. He used to dream of having an empty diary and being able to just potter in the garden.

One idyllic summer I was finally invited to the most talked-about party of the season in the notorious Cotswold Golden Triangle – actually more like a twelve-sided something or other. Driving around to various neighbouring properties, like Charlie and Rebekah's country residence, set on the vast estate of Charlie's family, or David and Samantha Cameron's house, just down the road from Lord and Lady Bamford's estate, was like being swallowed up by a period drama.

There is an unbroken run of stately homes, broken up only by field upon field, all framed by dry-stone walls, idyllic village greens and pretty cottages. There are hardly any ugly houses at all. Jeremy used to say you had to have a few council houses, otherwise where else would you get a cleaner from.

Anyhow, the summer party not to be missed was at the Gallaghers' house, no not the Oasis boys, but Tony Gallagher, an Irish builder done good, very good. I didn't get to explore his entire kingdom, but what I did see was literally fit for a king or a prime minister, some media moguls, a few rock-'n'-

roll characters and, of course, the aforementioned Brooks wedding.

Jeremy and I planned to camp out at the farm house. He'd arranged for his PA to get a new bed delivered with duvet, pillows and all, and I had packed my car with an essential survival kit: teabags, milk, sugar, kettle etc. along with a hoover to tackle all the dead flies which decorated the whole place, including the bath. It was actually great fun, and Jeremy said there weren't many girls that would endure this. I think he was right!

In fact, I think I really might be the only one who is prepared to hoover flies out of the bath before filling it with water from the kettle, then tip-toeing carefully on the clean patches of carpet before donning my party dress and high heels to go and meet the best of the best in the notorious Chipping Norton Set.

*   *   *   *

So, leaving behind our half-derelict house, we set off in a Ferrari or some other supercar that was difficult to get in and out of, especially as I was wearing a short dress and high heels. As a motoring journalist, Jeremy had at least one car a week delivered to wherever he was residing for him to test out before writing one of his notorious reviews. I wish we'd had something more suitable for country living, but it did not look out of place driving down the mile-or-so-long private, tree-lined drive. (The trees apparently cost around £250,000. There were a lot of them.)

My nerves kicked in a little as we pulled up in front of a huge manor house/palace to be met by the butler, who had controversially been poached by the Gallaghers from Lord and Lady Bamford. The Bamfords are head of the JCB empire and Daylesford Organic, but more about them later. Much more. There were no simple neighbourly arguments out here of music being played too loudly or footballs constantly being kicked into roses; here, it was more about butlers and helipads.

With glass of champagne in hand, I was led through to the garden by Jeremy to meet the billionaire owner of the house. I had heard so much about Tony and his wife Rita and their great summer party, which was one of the highlights of Jeremy's party calendar; that and the Gallaghers' Christmas party, which included a carol service in their very own chapel within the grounds.

Tony was a larger-than-life character, a far cry from his humble beginnings in Ireland. Jeremy had told me he was always meticulously turned out and he did not disappoint on this beautiful summer evening. He was the polar opposite of our hero Mr Clarkson. Tony had the crispest of shirts on; I hate ironing and I really didn't know you could get a shirt to look that good. In comparison to Mr C's tombstone display of teeth, you needed sunglasses when Tony flashed a smile. He reminded me of a seventies game-show host, and was as hospitable as one, oozing with charisma. Also, as I was soon to find out, a very generous 'feeder' of alcohol, just like the real game-show host, Chris Evans.

After a warm welcome from Tony and his wife Rita, we found the mightily relieved Rebekah and Charlie, who had been found not guilty, chatting to the Camerons and Claire and Alex James, also famous for a good party. In fact, festivals at their Cotswolds farm were as famous for their cheese as for a good night out. Alex James is the charming 'bad boy' from Britpop band Blur.

I'd always liked the public persona of the Camerons, as portrayed in their various TV and other media appearances. But they really are genuinely lovely and, within ten minutes, I found myself chatting to Sam Cam about bra or no bra – we had both opted, on this glorious summer evening, for no bra. We went from having a good old girly giggle to tears as we talked about our special-needs sons. The loss and grief of their dear Ivan was still very raw. And so there I was – I hadn't seen this coming at all – talking tits and tears with the then prime minister's good lady.

At all the extraordinary events I went to with Jeremy, he was more often than not a VIP guest, and this evening was no exception. We were placed at the top table and I was seated close to Jeremy, the PM, Sam Cam and next to model Cara Delevingne's father, Charles, the quintessential English socialite, descended from a few honourables and viscounts, a great laugh and a terrible flirt.

It was all going swimmingly, until my head started swimming. Oh, that was a scary moment. I'm sitting next to the prime minister, trying to keep up with the discussion he and JC were having on Russia; Putin was about to invade Crimea, in an earlier attempt to take over Ukraine. The alcohol was flowing in a way that you really weren't sure how much you'd drunk because your wine glass was always magically full. That magic was created by the very best of serving staff, who were so attentive that no more than an inch of the top of your glass would ever be showing. They were expert stealth decanters of wine, and they were dangerous.

Mr Cameron has been blamed for a lot since his rapid exit from number ten and I don't agree with it all, but I very much do blame him for what happened next at the summer party of the year. The stealth drink waiters switched to a blatant attack, offering tequila shots. The PM went straight in for one and to be polite, and because of my chronic FOMO (Fear Of Missing Out), I went right in alongside him. The tequilas were elegantly served, like everything else that night, on bespoke wooden mini-boards loaded with lemon and salt. And there it was, another most memorable moment as I downed what I'm sure was the finest tequila with my new best mate, 'Dave'.

Finest or not, that tequila had the same effect on me as a lethal injection on your beloved ancient dog, who can barely stand up, so you've finally made the heart-breaking but brave decision to end it all humanely, and you watch as dear Rover silently and swiftly sinks into the deepest of sleeps.

I fought it so hard, fuelled by sheer fear of utterly disgracing myself, as I was sure my head was about to hit the table as the tequila did its worst. My mind has taken me to that epic scene in *The Wolf of Wall Street* when Leonardo DiCaprio crawls down the steps to climb into his supercar while, in his mind, he's suavely gliding down the club steps, entering his car and coolly exiting the sweeping driveway of his private club.

I wasn't quite as bad as that, I don't think, but I had to hang on to the backs of chairs as I made a hasty retreat, or as hasty as I could, to the nearest bathroom where – I'm totally ashamed and embarrassed, but will tell you anyway – another scene from a movie, a horror movie, played out. Just as I managed to close behind me the door of the largest goddamn cloakroom I'd ever seen, I failed miserably to reach the loo, which was a good five yards from the door, so projectile vomited with such force that I literally redecorated the entire enormous room!

Oh. My. God! The good news was that I instantly sobered up. The bad news was that I had to somehow clean the whole place up. I must have been in there for ages wiping the whole floor and all the walls with reams of loo roll. Honestly, I doubt you have, and I hope you haven't and never will see anything like it. As I've mentioned before, I am not good at drinking, but in those days I just kept on trying, even though I had these catastrophic reactions.

After making sure there was nothing sinister left on my shoes or dress – thank God the force of the projectile was strong and I had miraculously missed most of myself, save for the tips of my toes – I splashed myself with cold water, sprayed some of the luxury perfume on offer and set off to re-join the VIP table. To my disappointment, the PM had been called away as the Russian crisis was heating up. Thank God Dave was made of stronger stuff than me or his time in office may have ended even more dramatically.

I don't remember getting back to the farm, or how we did so, but, despite our most basic of rooms, I slept well and, when I woke, Jeremy had been out for the Sunday papers and we sat around a trestle table in our shit kitchen downing coffee and bacon rolls. Just another day in the extraordinary life of Jeremy Clarkson.

6

Back in London Town

Second in the league table of wall-to-wall celebrity parties, after Sir David Tang's most star-studded events, were Jimmy Carr's celebtastic soirées.

Jimmy's home, as I've briefly described before, was literally purpose-built for entertaining. It has an indoor pool, a tennis court, enough garden terrace to host a decent-sized BBQ – I mean, the size BBQ you might see at a small festival – a pool table, a table-tennis table, a full range of sweet dispensers for you to load up from before you sit down very comfortably in the mini-cinema. It was fantastic, and so were Jimmy and his girlfriend Caroline at hosting these regular themed nights.

The one I can remember most clearly was an American-themed BBQ, celebrating the Fourth of July, Independence Day. The house was decorated with stars and stripes, the napkins etc. were all sporting the American flag, and the BBQ was loaded with hot dogs and burgers with every relish you could imagine available to liven them up. But the guests were what really made these parties. Jimmy's phone must have been so hot with whose numbers he had stored on it. It would be an absolute corker for a phone hacker to find.

We had many nights there, often staying for only a couple of hours as Jimmy's parties were typically on a Monday or a Tuesday and Jeremy would be working the next day. He was also, strangely, not a big fan of them, perhaps because he was so often not the biggest star there?

This particular evening, it was packed. Richard and Mindy Hammond were there, a first for them. I think Richard had just been on one of Jimmy's quiz shows and he just joined the rest of the cast on Jimmy's phone. Also there were Rachel Riley from *8 Out of 10 Cats Does Countdown*; Hugh Grant and his girlfriend (now wife), Anna; ex-*Blue Peter* presenter, Konnie Huq, who is also the co-writer of some of *Black Mirror*, which her husband, Charlie Brooker, created (Charlie's satirical *Newswipe* is one of my favourite shows).

The house was jam-packed with many more household names: Tess Daly, Vernon Kay, Holly Willoughby, Jamie and Louise Redknapp, James Corden and billionaire property developer Nick Candy, there with his wife, Australian soap and pop star, Holly Valance. There were sports stars whose names I can't quite remember, a harem of Hugh Grant's exes – Jemima Khan and Liz Hurley. Well, not quite a harem, and Hugh just made light of it by saying, 'It's always fun when all your ex-girlfriends are at a party.' It was Anna, his girlfriend of the moment, that I felt sorry for. The others were seemingly all quite comfortable in each other's company.

Did I mention Hugh Grant earlier on? After my fleeting first meeting with him at the film club, I was yet again a little too excited to be in his presence, but I think I managed to hide it. I actually got talking to Anna, who is so grounded; we spoke about living unconventional and complicated lives. At the time, she and Hugh had at least one child together and Hugh had two from a previous short-lived relationship, but he plays a big part in all his children's lives. Hugh was lovely: so utterly charming and very funny. He asked me what I did, if I worked in TV too. I replied, 'I'm actually probably the least qualified person to be here.'

Very kindly, he said, 'I don't believe that.'

'Well, I'm mainly a mother,' I said.

'The most important job,' he replied.

At this point, I had totally forgiven him for messing around with a prostitute (a scandal in America he had been caught up in that had made headlines) and my crush just got way bigger.

It was also the night of another huge introduction, yet another very daunting one, to Liz Murdoch, daughter of Rupert, and a major media executive, involved with many production companies such as Shine, Endemol and 21st Century Fox, but also one of the key members of the Chipping Norton Set. At the time, she was still married to Matthew Freud, PR guru and son of Sir Clement Freud, grandson of Sigmund Freud – God knows what *he* would have made of the egos and alter egos at this fascinating house party.

However, Liz, in the same way that the equally powerful Rebekah Brooks had been, was very humble and socially anxious too. I found her very endearing, completely the opposite of what I had expected, which had been a hard-nosed businesswoman. If those traits were there at all, she hid them well. Jeremy later told me that she was having a terrible time with her husband Matthew, which perhaps explained her fragility.

I felt more and more comfortable in this strange world that, from the outside, appears to be so glamorous, and something that many people would love to be involved in, but it was like being in a parallel universe. It was undeniably fun, but all quite superficial and I longed for some normality, as did Jeremy, but he was well and truly caught up in the chaos of marriage breakdown and the increasing pressure of more and more work. All these parties were a good distraction, but he didn't seem capable of stopping and creating any normality. I was grateful for my downtime back at my home with my boy and all my animals.

We enjoyed many nights at Jimmy and Caroline's. My second best moment, after meeting Hugh Grant, was arriving just behind Sir Elton John and his husband David Furnish. Jeremy and I joined them in the grand entrance hall where the staff were taking their coats. We politely exchanged nods and said, 'Evening' to one another, then David turned to Sir Elton and asked, 'Do you need the toilet, Elton?' I wasn't expecting that! It was as if he was Elton's carer, which I guess he probably is to some extent. And that does sum up the situation quite well. Yes, it is very glamorous and exciting in that world, but, at the end of the day, all those celebs are just human beings like the rest of us.

7

Hugh Grant Wants My Number!!!

Warning: If you are not a fan of Hugh Grant, you may not be interested in this. On the other hand, you may become his biggest fan after reading how and why he asked me out.

The morning after the night before at Jimmy's, I had headed home to Hertfordshire and Planet Normal. Until I got a call from Jeremy to say that Hugh Grant had messaged him asking for my contact details, as he wanted to invite me to something. Oh My F***ing God, really!!?? And there I was, back in that parallel universe.

It turned out Hugh had co-written a book. Well, I say written; in actual fact it didn't have many words in it at all, as it was specifically for children and adults with learning difficulties and comprised illustrations depicting scenes which the reader could interpret in their own way with guidance from a carer or parent. The book was one of a series created by Baroness Sheila Hollins, whom Hugh had befriended through Hacked Off, the campaign group for a free and accountable press in the UK. Both have been victims of press abuse. Baroness Hollins also has a son with autism. She had endured terrible press intrusion when her daughter was stabbed whilst pregnant and walking with her young son, the stuff of nightmares. Baroness Hollins's daughter was left paralysed from her injuries and I shouldn't say any more than that because that's exactly what Baroness Hollins doesn't want. I am in awe of her for rising above tragedy and wrongdoing to continue to help those who have difficulty with understanding the world and its rules.

At Jimmy's party, when we had discussed the perils of parenting, Hugh had clearly taken on board the fact that my son had learning difficulties and thought that he and I might like to come to the launch of his book, *The Drama Club*. I was so touched, but then slightly panicked, at the thought of taking Alfie, my son, to Sadler's Wells in London where the launch was being celebrated with a one-off performance of the story, starring Hugh and the children and adults from the Baked Bean Drama Theatre Company for actors with learning disabilities.

I was now chatting with my new friend, Hugh, by email and so asked if it was at all possible to bring one of Alfie's carers with me. And soon enough, we were in front-row seats within touching distance of my screen heartthrob. Definitely did not see that coming!! Nor could I have predicted the humour and understanding Hugh had for Alfie when he lost his patience with what he deemed a not-so-interesting play and unleashed one of his high-pitched protest screams at the stage. Hugh just raised an eyebrow and looked on sympathetically with an air of amusement, rather than any kind of disgust, which is how so many react to the seemingly inappropriate behaviour of these complicated, sensitive beings. Alfie's dear carer, Corrina, promptly asked Alfie if he would like to leave the theatre and left me, falling ever more in love with Hugh, as he acted out the story with the rest of the cast.

It got even better at the after-show party when Hugh, after delivering a humorous and emotive speech with Baroness Hollins, made a big effort to find me in the crowd and insisted on meeting Alfie and Corrina. Now, that was a night. Quite an emotional one for me as it was the first time I'd dared to take Alfie to a theatre and, despite his little outburst, I had managed to engage him in everything that was going on. He loved the lights and the set changes, but most of all he loved the lifts in the foyer. I teased Hugh that these had been, unfortunately, the highlight for Alfie. Hugh took it in good humour, replying that the lifts were not the worst thing he'd been upstaged by.

It turned out that Hugh had grown up with someone with learning difficulties, a child of a friend of his mother. With his insight into how tricky life can be for adults with a learning disability, Hugh set up the Fynvola Foundation, named after his mother. The foundation supports a residential home for adults with disabilities.

To add to Hugh's little-known litany of saintly doings, he had also made a dream come true for Baroness Hollins's son, to have a small part in one of his films. Hugh flew him out to New York to join him on set. I couldn't be more in love with him, and I shall always be so grateful for the very special opportunity to introduce Alfie to the theatre. And I was glad that the never-ending demands of Jezza's work had meant that he couldn't attend, which had left me to enjoy drooling over Hugh alone.

8

Time for a Break

At last Jeremy had planned a holiday for just the two of us, finally slowing the crazy pace, which I had begun to wonder just how he kept up. Our favourite country whilst touring was South Africa and we decided it would be the perfect place for a holiday. We could travel overnight in the comfort of first class and arrive with no jet lag as it is in pretty much the same time zone as the UK. It's also one of the very few countries where Jeremy doesn't get recognised too much.

Some of Jeremy's numerous contacts found an amazing private home for our exclusive use. The only mistake the big man made was using the company who ran the *Top Gear Live* tour, which therefore assumed that it must be real, top-end luxury that was wanted, as that is what he demands whilst touring. The truth is that Jeremy is fundamentally a Yorkshireman and doesn't really like parting with his cash; even more so when he was trying to hide his spending from his ex-wife, from whom he was newly separated.

We were met at the airport by one of our usual tour drivers in the standard issue top-of-the-range Range Rover. I don't know how this was all arranged, but there was usually a small army jumping into action to meet the big man's demands. We were soon parking in the basement garage of a stunning modern mansion set into the rocks, looking out over the ocean in an exclusive suburb of Cape Town.

We took the lift from the garage to arrive in a vast living and dining area of the sort that (expert designer) Kevin McCloud would burst with enthusiasm over. To the front was floor-to-ceiling glass to allow you to take in the sunrise and sunset over the Atlantic. It had a full-sized bar leading out to the outdoor dining area, sun terrace and pool.

To the rear was the indoor dining area which incorporated part of the rock face and an internal tropical garden, which blended into the towering rocks beyond, forming what I'd call the thirteenth, fourteenth and fifteenth apostles. (The Twelve Apostles is the name given to the famous rock formations just beyond Table Mountain.) More floor-to-ceiling glass walls formed the back of the house and one edge of the dining area formed a balcony edged with glass that overlooked another indoor garden where a full-size palm tree and other greenery grew up from the ground floor. It would have made a great set for any James Bond movie or the *Thunderbirds* HQ, or a South African version of the Eden Project. The ground floor had further bedrooms, an office and a gym. We never went there.

The main bedroom was huge, with a ceiling studded with thousands of star lights and more floor-to-ceiling glass leading out to an infinity pool surrounded by glass walls so you had the feeling of being able to swim out to sea. It was incredible.

We had Clinton, our familiar tour driver, at our disposal so we began our adventure by heading to the local supermarket to stock up. That may surprise you, but without the endless demands for selfies Jeremy loved to food shop and I loved just to share those 'normal couple' moments, choosing foodie treats and stocking up the bar for our first solo escape.

Unfortunately, his anonymity was short-lived. On day one, we decided to drive ourselves and give Clinton the day off in order to have more privacy whilst we ventured along the dramatic coastline in search of a quiet spot to enjoy a romantic picnic on the beach. (Yes, the blustering, bombastic orangutan of a man could be very romantic.) We thought we'd cracked it. The beachside car park had just half a dozen cars in. It looked promising. After parking, Jeremy said, 'Stay there, I'll check for crowds.' We couldn't see the actual beach to know if it was full of towel-to-towel sunbathers and surfers. It was accessed down a steep set of steps. He set off, hiding his trademark mad hair (he had some then) with a baseball cap and trying to hide some of his giant face with sunglasses.

It wasn't long before he came back looking happy, although out of breath. Jeremy doesn't do walking at the best of times and a near-vertical set of steps was a challenge for the forty-plus-a-day smoker. A family had just arrived and as Jeremy crossed the car park and as the excited kids made their way to the beach, they suddenly shrieked, 'It's Jeremy Clarkson!' And that was the end of that.

His genius disguise had failed and, although there really were only half a dozen parked cars and the shrieking children had moved on, Jeremy had been triggered. He hated being famous, a victim of his own great success. He went into a bit of a diva strop and would take no rational advice from me. We were off. The mood was tense, but we persevered and found ourselves a rather special spot amongst the giant rounded boulders at the other end of the bay, where we could enjoy our picnic alone, albeit being rather uncomfortable, not stretched out on the soft, golden sand, and after a small mountaineering expedition. You really can't have it all. Although we did get to watch the sunset over the majestic Twelve Apostles.

*   *   *   *

Jeremy loves the great outdoors, which is probably apparent from all the *Top Gear* and *Grand Tour* films. He is a secret twitcher, a bird spotter, something he and Adrian Gill shared a passion for. He loved a good sunset, something that was a big feature on this holiday, including one that David Attenborough would have been delighted with, as we sat on a hotel terrace watching a huge pod of dolphins play around in the Atlantic beyond.

Of course, a Clarkson holiday wouldn't be right without a big night out and we were invited by the South African director of the *Top Gear Live* tour to dinner at the hippest beach bar/ restaurant in the area. And, of course, it would not be a proper Clarkson holiday night out if there wasn't a fellow celebrity there. John Bishop was the celeb of choice.

John was actually not drinking at the time as he was training for a marathon or something, but, as you know, he is naturally funny and is, as I had the pleasure to find out, a genuinely lovely guy. Our *Top Gear Live* director, Paul, was not going to be running a marathon any time soon and was ready to get stuck in to the cocktails and all.

The venue did not disappoint, right on the beach, where we had a prime spot in one of the large day-beds in a cool lounge area on the edge of the beach. Paul, bless him, who has since sadly passed, was slightly over-excited about his special guests and sank a few too many beverages far too quickly. He had to be scraped up from the day-bed (not easy, as he was over six feet tall and easily that in circumference, too, built like a heavyweight rugby player). His long-suffering PA bundled him into a car, apologised to us and left us to enjoy the rest of the evening.

John left shortly afterwards as one can drink only so many soft drinks whilst spectating others getting smashed. Jeremy had managed to confirm yet again the theory of six degrees of separation. It was bad enough that wherever we went most people knew him from off the telly, but Jeremy also actually knew a hell of a lot of people and, on a trip back from the loo, he said he'd bumped into a bunch of guys who used to drink in his old Fulham haunts when he was just Jeremy Clarkson, not that man from the telly and so, yet again, we were in it for the long haul, shots and all.

We did not see much of the next day, but had some memories of yet another great night out. I had partially succeeded in getting the big man to relax a little, but it was certainly no detox and we were soon back on the plane home to hit the ground running for an increasingly crazy schedule.

I often visited the *Top Gear* track and studio hanger down at Dunsfold, often in a work capacity, and once we had been outed as a couple, Jeremy loved having me there for moral support. Studio day, when they filmed with the live audience and filmed 'Star in a Reasonably Priced Car' was full on. Jeremy, James and Richard would get there first thing in the morning and go through the script, making any changes and rehearsing.

The 'stars' would then spend a good few hours being trained by The Stig out on the track before they put in their timed lap. The more competitive they were, the more time they tried to persuade the crew to give them to practise. I was lucky enough to meet the legend that is Tom Cruise and the beauty that is Cameron Diaz, both incredibly grounded people. When Jeremy introduced me and was stumbling over his words as to what to call me – girlfriend, partner or whatever – I said I was his mother. They all roared with laughter.

There was a classic Tom Cruise hero moment when a gust of wind took out a gazebo. As it lifted off, Tom was first on the scene, pulling it back. It was one of those moments that kind of froze in time as we all stood back in slight shock that he would bother with such a menial but nevertheless heroic task. Everyone was slightly embarrassed that he'd reacted the quickest and got there first. He is a legend.

Tom and Cameron said that they had had the best day and were reluctant to leave. Their huge entourage was not so keen to stick around as they had to get them to the *Knight and Day* première in London.

That was an epic day in *Top Gear* history. The boys, Andy Wilman and the crew were so chuffed. They couldn't quite believe that the show had achieved such a status that they could get A-listers to battle it out on track and not want to leave.

*　*　*　*

I had a few filming experiences with the amazing crew who pulled together all the incredible locations, cars and stunts. I had the pleasure of watching James, Jeremy and The Stig rip up Twickenham's hallowed ground whilst playing 'car rugby' with Kia C'eeds, of former reasonably-priced-car fame, being used as speedy backs, while up front, Kia Sportages served as the hard-man forwards. The Stig was the referee, in a police car, of course.

The power the show had towards the end of Clarkson's reign was incredible. Pretty much anyone you spoke to wanted to be involved, so when someone put the call through to Twickenham, the officials were easily persuaded to let cars rip up their sacred ground. In actual fact, the proposal was put forward when the ground was due to be completely replaced, but it was still quite a big ask.

In the same way that others close to him did, I noticed that Jeremy's expectations and demands were getting a little out of hand, as was his tolerance if he didn't get what he wanted. I was the only one who dared to put him in his place, while at the same time keeping him reasonably happy, so Andy Wilman liked having me around to help keep him on an even keel.

One such occasion was when Clarkson, Hammond and May all took part in a twenty-four-hour race at Silverstone. A lot of people think that the three boys don't actually endure the full challenge that gets broadcast, and that there is clever editing involved. I can confirm that just as in any twenty-four-hour race, Jeremy, James and Richard were there for the duration, and more. I had been asked to look after them whilst they weren't on track. They had a Winnebago (large luxury motorhome) where they could get their heads down in between stints on the track.

I also got my first cameo role as masseuse for The Stig. We set up a massage table above the pit garage and The Stig lay down – fully clothed and with his helmet on, of course – while I ran my magic hands over him. Despite all of us finding the scene very amusing, it didn't make the cut, and that was the end of my acting career.

That was a full-on, intense shoot, although certainly not their toughest. It never ceased to amaze me what they could endure, but I did worry about Jeremy especially, as he obviously didn't look after himself; in fact, quite the opposite. He defies medical science.

9

Fantasy Island

It must be time for another party – April 2014, Mustique.

As I was ever more closely embraced into Jeremy's inner circle of friends, JC and I would be invited to more of the intimate dinner parties at Jeremy's friends' houses; sometimes Jeremy would socialise in my humble world, but that wasn't very often. He really wasn't too keen on my social circle. I don't think there were enough titles amongst my friends and he once quipped that 'none of them did drugs'. Slightly childish, more akin to a teenage spat, but, unfortunately, he did behave like a stroppy teenager on numerous occasions.

Anyhow, back in his mad world I enjoyed the more relaxed suppers in the comfort and privacy of his friends' homes, where there was no fear of paparazzi and no relentless demands for selfies. Belle Robinson, whom I had first met with her husband at the private members' club in Hertford Place, had sadly split up from her husband John, but had found comfort in her new man, Hamish. He was a City man, but best of all a fantastic dinner party guest, a great raconteur and a great performer of party tricks. We bonded as a foursome and Belle was the perfect hostess, serving up home-cooked gastronomic delights in her cosy, cool Kensington flat.

I had one very memorable birthday supper at Belle's when guests included Rory Bremner, Richard E. Grant and Bryan Ferry. Bryan arrived late, but then proceeded to lead the way in singing happy birthday to me.

Bizarrely, I met Jeremy's latest girlfriend, Lisa, one night when Jeremy couldn't be there as he was at *The Sun*'s Military Awards dinner. I remember her well, even though she looked quite different to how she does now. What I do remember was that she was even taller than me, and I'm six foot, although she did have incredibly high heels on. She kept me cornered for a while, fascinated to hear what Jeremy was like.

Her boyfriend at the time was very good friends with BBC executive Danny Cohen, who had brought about the end of Jeremy's career with the BBC, so I cut the conversation short. There's that six degrees of separation playing out again. Small – and weird – world.

Our friendship with Belle and Hamish grew and we were invited to join them on a holiday to Mustique, where Belle and John, her ex-husband, had not one, but two houses. And when I say houses, they were more like luxury boutique hotels. I was about to experience the unique and private island of the very, very rich and the seriously famous.

* * * *

For those of you who don't know, Mustique is a private island in the nation of St Vincent and the Grenadines in the West Indies. It was bought by a good friend of Princess Margaret, Lord Glenconner, Colin Tennant, for just £45,000 in 1958. That amount of money would buy you only about a week to stay there now. The princess bought her own plot and, as is well documented, holidayed and partied there for many years.

I have read that Mustique's numerous, fantastical villas were designed by a British theatre set designer, which doesn't surprise me. I have been lucky enough to have dined and partied in several of them, one set right on the beach, owned by Lawrence Stroll, Canadian billionaire, best known now as the father of F1 driver Lance Stroll and the owner of the Aston Martin F1 team. Lawrence's father played a big role in the success of brands such as Tommy Hilfiger, Pierre Cardin and Ralph Lauren, taking them to Canada, and beyond.

The style of the Strolls' palatial villa is Indian-influenced and is of mind-blowing proportions, with its own private beach – again, a bit more like a boutique hotel than a home. The guest of honour at their party was none other than Bryan Adams, but the favourite was Mr Clarkson, as budding young racing driver Lance was desperate to meet him. The desperation was unfortunately not mutual. Jeremy can be embarrassingly aloof when he's really not interested in someone who is interested in him.

Belle's second property on Mustique was more of a compound of Roman villas, fit for an emperor. Each bedroom suite was an individual villa within the grounds. Another home was like a palace, set on the top of the island. I can't even remember whose it was, but they threw a very good party – a sit-down dinner for about 150, who were easily accommodated in the palatial dining room.

To get to Mustique was quite a journey, but well worth it. We flew to a larger Caribbean island – Barbados, I think – where they had a big enough airport to cope with normal-sized commercial planes. On arrival, we were guided to a shed to wait for our small plane, a six-seater. As we sat and waited for an annoyingly long and very hot time, Jeremy said, 'I bet we'll bump into someone I know.' He had his head buried in a book, but I was enjoying people-watching. A man, who looked very familiar, entered the room and I clocked him spotting Jeremy. Nothing unusual in that, but as predicted, when Jeremy lifted his head from his book, he immediately acknowledged the rather good-looking chap. The man came across and shook Jeremy's hand, there was a short exchange about travelling to Mustique, then the vaguely familiar man went off to get a drink. Jeremy turned to me as I looked questioningly at him, and whispered, 'Bryan Adams.' Wow, not just any old Bryan: Bryan 'Rock Star' Adams!! I couldn't believe I hadn't realised. I guess it was just a classic case of 'out of context'.

Not long afterwards, we were squashing ourselves into a tiny plane, without Bryan; he was booked on another. Only teeny-tiny planes can land on Mustique, and I was about to find out why. After a short, very picturesque flight, island-spotting in the turquoise waters below, we started our descent, which was rather nerve-racking as I couldn't see any land, let alone a runway.

Then we were really low and the land looked way too close. Still, there was no sign of a runway. All of a sudden we flew over a rise in the land and just the other side was the smallest airport and runway I'd ever seen. It was the prettiest airport I'd ever seen too. As we disembarked in paradise, I was half expecting a dwarf in a white suit to appear, saying 'Welcome to Fantasy Island.' (Do you remember that seventies American fantasy drama of the same name?)

Arrivals was an open-fronted palm-roofed area attached to a small wooden building adorned with bright pink bougainvillaea. Our bags were simply carried by the ground staff to a table and our passports were checked with no sense of authority at all.

We weren't met by a dwarf, but instead our delightful hosts for the week, Belle and Hamish, also rather embarrassingly, by

David Ross, whom I'd dated in the past. That was a surprise. I thought he must be a guest of Mark Cecil, who had introduced me to him, but I later learnt David had his own house on the island. I kept my head down. He and Jeremy had once had a little battle for my attention in a London nightclub. Let's just say there wasn't any love lost between them.

After breezing through immigration – when there are just five of you, it doesn't take long – we were shown to our transport, a golf buggy. Not Jeremy's favourite vehicle, but that's all there was on the island in order to maintain the instant, enforced air of calm. There were to be no flash motors speeding around.

Bouncing along in the golf buggy, we passed the immaculate riding school, full of picture-perfect ponies, and the school house, like something out of the TV series *Little House on the Prairie*, whilst looking out for giant tortoises, of which there are hundreds on the island. I really did feel like I'd landed on a fantasy island.

We soon arrived at Belle's preferred island home, and I totally agreed with her choice. In fact, after visiting a dozen or so other homes on the island, out of all the fantasy villas, Hibiscus, as Belle's villa is called, was my absolute favourite.

The villa had a charming, luxurious but not opulent feel. It was beautifully stylish and catered for your every holiday need, with a beautiful pool overlooking the sea below, surrounded by tropical plants and stunning bougainvillaea. It had a veranda, perfect for afternoon tea or pre-dinner G and Ts, and a huge indoor/outdoor dining area set in the centre of the property, which created an idyllic quadrangle, framed at the back by the rockface, a natural wall, garlanded with tropical flora, with a central water feature to top it all off. Our suite had a huge bathroom and we had our own private terrace with a plunge pool. It was just heaven and I couldn't wait to relax.

No time to relax, though, on this notoriously hedonistic party island. I soon learnt that if you don't arrive home from Mustique feeling like you need a holiday, you haven't had a holiday on Mustique.

I found the schedule quite overwhelming – 'overweighting' too! The day started with a full breakfast at which we discussed what time and where we would be meeting for lunch and what evening entertainment was planned.

*　*　*　*

I was very lucky to visit Mustique three times and enjoyed every minute. I just would have loved to have had a few more minutes of relaxation. But that was never gonna happen, being with the ultimate party animal that is Jezza, especially surrounded by some of his best partners in crime.

We lunched at other millionaires' mansions – Camilla Sainsbury's vast modern minimalistic home that would suit a Bond villain for a lair and the Cecils', among others. (Mark Cecil used to go out with a friend of mine and introduced me to David Ross. I also discovered that David's grandfather was in the same masonic lodge as mine. Please don't mistake me for being in the same bracket though; my grandfather was a hospital manager, David's was a wealthy businessman.) That's a big sidetrack, sorry. Mark Cecil originally trained as a doctor, but went on to retrain for a career in investment management; he has recently been appointed by Boris Johnson as a trustee of the National Portrait Gallery. I'm going to forget the six-degree thing in this scenario and go for full separation from that connection.

Moving swiftly on, Mark's house was old-school Mustique – colonial, but with a contemporary twist. It had a huge wooden wraparound veranda and an open-air dining pavilion. Once used by Prince William and Kate Middleton, it was quite understated, but still very luxurious, and great for a party. It's called Aurora if you ever fancy treating yourself and some of your nearest and dearest. God, if I were super-wealthy, that's what I'd do.

My favourite lunches by far were the ones at the beach, and I don't mean a rug with a picnic hamper. In keeping with the millionaire lifestyle, any resident could book their own private beach area, complete with pitched-roofed open shelters, where the host's staff could dress the tables with linen and decorate them with matching bunting. Cutlery and glasses and everything else required, such as flowers, ice, wine coolers, all the luxury dining equipment that was available in the villa, was whizzed down by golf buggy and, as if by magic, a delicious three-course meal was served up with buckets of wine and beer.

I have a picture of Jeremy on the island with the largest bottle of organic rosé I have ever seen, about two feet tall! And that would have been flown in specially from the Bamfords' Daylesford vineyard. The lunches were my favourite. I think a boozy lunch followed by an afternoon snooze is the best holiday treat, as did Jeremy. Unfortunately, the evening parties were a big draw and, although optional, the big man did not like to let anyone down by not showing up. They were, of course, great fun too, but a little more dangerous.

10

I Am a Rolling Stone

A while back, I watched a Rolling Stones documentary broadcast in honour of the passing of Charlie Watts – I was going to write 'sad' here, but it's not really, is it? He had a very full life and from all I've heard, was a lovely guy, who has just gone up in my estimation as it turns out that, in addition to being a brilliant drummer, he was also a huge horse and dog lover.

Anyway, as I was watching the documentary, I was realising not only just how old The Rolling Stones all are now, but also that I'd had little idea of most of their achievements, and their anarchic life, because I had been just a little girl at the time, a very uncoordinated one at that. That girl would never have imagined, in her wildest of dreams, that one day she would dance with Mick Jagger and I mean WITH, as a dancing partner.

Jagger was one of the first incredibly famous and wealthy part-time residents of Mustique. No doubt his hedonistic lifestyle would have been full on in the luxury and guaranteed privacy of this incredible, surreal, beautiful, idyllic Caribbean island.

When I had the honour of meeting him, he was in his latter years, a quite wizened, tiny old man. He was shyly and quietly sitting at the end of the dining table at one of the many extraordinary dining experiences that I had whilst staying at Hibiscus.

The dining table in the courtyard had been extended to seat twenty-two of us. It had been beautifully laid, with artisan plates and locally sourced, tropically influenced linen napkins and beautiful table ornaments. It was adorned with sweet-smelling fresh flowers and glittering with candles, silver cutlery and crystal glasses. Truly, it was a sight to behold, like a scene from *Dallas* or *Dynasty*, or contemporary al fresco dining at Highclere Castle, where *Downtown Abbey* is set.

Of course, to top the whole scene off, there were beautiful dinner guests from other exquisite houses cleverly nestled out of sight of any others all over the island. Everyone was casually but stylishly and expensively dressed in linen, silk, gold and diamonds – except for me. In stark contrast, on my single-mother, part-time income, I was the odd one out, but I've always had an eye for a bargain and, so I'm told, have good taste and style.

I was wearing a Ghost dress that I'd bought in a discount store for about £50, instead of the £250 it should have cost, and I'd paired it with sandals from Next, which is where I get most of my shoes as I have exceptionally large feet and Next do a great range in huge shoes, which means I don't have to put myself through the misery of shoe shopping, looking at all the shoes I'd really love, but can't have. A simple click online once I've spotted the best of the limited choice and my shoes would be delivered to my door, pretty much guaranteed to fit. And if not, one phone call and the ill-fitting shoes would be swiftly collected, without drama and with no sore feet.

Jeremy always said I was a clothes-horse and that anything I wore looked good, but that was before I'd been on several holidays in Mustique, which is no good for most people's waistlines. There were a few exceptions: the younger generation, not yet prone to middle-aged spread, and the model types, like Malin Jefferies, the Swedish model married to Tim Jefferies, a real man about town – art dealer and gallery owner and grandson of the founder of Green Shield Stamps and Argos.

Tim is known for running the super-A-list, ultra-glam summer party of the Serpentine Gallery – the one where Princess Diana turned up shortly after the public announcement of Charles admitting to adultery. She famously wowed everyone in that stunning, short, black, off-the-shoulder chiffon number. The perfect fingers up to old Charlie boy.

Tickets to the event, in aid of charity, cost hundreds of pounds, and you have to apply for them. Tim is known for his extensive connections with beautiful, famous women, and he's dated most of them. Jeremy was a great fan of his, also probably a tad jealous of his dating history. Tim's little black book reportedly includes Claudia Schiffer, Naomi Campbell, Elle Macpherson, Sophie Dahl and Kylie Minogue, to name just a few.

However, at this time, he was clearly in love and had married Malin, who, despite having given birth in the recent past, was in top shape, as was fellow model and friend, Gabriela Peacock, now known for her nutrition advice. She is renowned for helping socialites to balance their hedonistic, toxic lives with the odd detox and counterbalancing dietary habits. Can you believe she even persuaded Jezza to sign up to a programme with her? Well, you would believe it if you saw her, knowing that Jeremy never turns down a bit of attention from a beautiful woman. I'm not sure it was the best move for Gabriela to try to use Jezza's profile to raise hers! Jeremy is not exactly a poster boy for healthy living!

Gabriela also had young children. She was married to a hedge-fund manager, David Peacock, whom I'd actually met before, as he worked with a very old friend of mine at J P Morgan – six degrees is never far away, but I must say I was blown away that it kept working in these elite social circles. I've gone off on a tangent again, easily done when there's so much to tell, but back to my outfit, cobbled together from a few bargains. I remember I was also wearing a set of layered necklaces with tiny crystals scattered along the delicate chains. A guest, who I later found out was a famous women's clothing designer, complimented me on my jewels, but mistakenly assumed they must be diamonds. (So famous I can't remember her name! I think it might have been Amanda Wakeley. She does have a Mustique wedding-dress collection, so that would make sense.) I laughed. 'I wish! They do a good job though, don't they?' I never really longed for diamonds. A few of my friends were amazed that I hadn't demanded any from millionaire Clarkson, but not only did I not have a great desire for them, he's a typically tight Yorkshireman!

Back to Mick (Jagger), whom I'm sure you're more interested in hearing about. After a wonderfully delicious meal rustled up by a team of chefs and lovingly served by the charming, loyal and local house staff, you might imagine that we would settle in to the sumptuous living room or look out to sea under the stars, reclining on the bespoke steamer chairs on the veranda with an after-dinner tipple. No, not here on Mustique, the island that never sleeps; it was time to party.

There was a staggered exit – there is never any rush whilst luxuriating on this island and each mind-blowingly stunning house, or palace, was open all hours. All guests were free to come and go as they wished, knowing there would always be a butler or head of housekeeping silently waiting, ready magically to appear if you needed them. Tonight, we were leaving my favourite house on the island. I often longed, on these party-packed holidays, to just relax and indulge in these perfect surroundings, but that was not the way life rolled here, or with Mr Clarkson for that matter, and my FOMO was happy to keep being fed.

Jeremy and I set off around midnight from the dedicated parking spot for the golf buggy which had been personally assigned to us. Even Jeremy enjoyed the simplicity of the golf buggies, but did, as you might expect, push the buggy to its limit. He also very much enjoyed the legalised drink-driving – as did I.

So off we whizzed like Fred and Wilma Flintstone to the very hedonistic 'holiday home' of world-renowned artist Marc Quinn. The house was rocking with a kind of techno music as we arrived, the illuminated dance-floor was set up al fresco – in fact, most of the property was al fresco – the dwelling itself was a very humble bungalow surrounded by a series of terraces, pergolas and unique nooks and crannies of cosy seating areas with a hippy chic, sixties vibe to the whole place.

Jeremy and I helped ourselves to the bottomless bowl of tropical punch and it wasn't long before I was up boogieing in my wedges, surrounded by an eclectic bunch, including Marc's stunning, Amazonian, Naomi Campbell-lookalike mistress (known and fully accepted by Marc's wife), our hostess Belle and her boyfriend Hamish, who was also throwing some shapes on the dance-floor. He was a real character, one of the best dinner guests you could have, a financial City guru of some kind by profession, with a straight image to match, but a great, engaging party guest, one of the funniest people I've ever met, who had an incredible talent for table magic. He once entertained us by pushing a cork back right inside a wine bottle and asking us to ponder how to get it out without breaking the bottle. He then, miraculously, with the help of a plastic carrier bag removed the cork back through the neck of the bottle.

Back to my epic dance-floor story. We were all sweating it out in the tropical heat, throwing ourselves around in a variety of fashions, surrounded by serious party people, many scuttling off to dark corners to inhale some special party magic.

Jeremy, not one for dancing, was tucked away in a corner with Jade Jagger, one of Mick's many offspring, whilst I was about to experience one of the highlights of my life with her father: a moment that literally millions of sixties wild childs would have dreamt of, perhaps hallucinated about. The one and truly only Mick Jagger faced up to me on the dance-floor – well, tried to – I was about six-foot three-inches in my wedges, but, as you know, the mighty presence of Mick was much bigger than his stature and through my drunken, fizzy, tingling body, I felt his magic.

OMG! There I was dancing with snake-hips himself, Mick Jagger!!! I feel the enormity of the moment as I write, especially after watching the scenes of thousands of crazed fans all over the world all clamouring for his attention in the documentary I'd watched, but at the time I was just loving dancing and the excitement I felt was like you would at any great night out with your best mates. In fact, Mick really reminded me of a good friend of my brother, someone I loved dancing with, so I felt quite at home.

What I was very aware of at the time was that this old man who had earlier been sitting quietly at the end of the dinner table, looking like he wasn't long for this world, could still move so incredibly well. I was really impressed, and could totally relate to how many younger women could be captivated by his energy. I was really flattered that he'd picked me out to dance with and was enjoying every second – until disaster struck. We were twisting away together, even more impressive for a man of his age especially when I, a couple of decades younger, twisted down … and got stuck.

And there it was, the most memorable dance-floor moment ever, when Mick Jagger had to pull me up off the floor. What a gentleman, what a legend. What an evening.

Not long after my dance-floor embarrassment, Jeremy decided to call time. I have no idea what time that was, but the party was thinning out a bit and I was definitely starting to fade. We headed off in our buggy in a blur. Next thing I knew, Jeremy had taken a corner a little too fast, nearly launching me out. I hung on somehow, but my clutch bag went flying, spilling all the contents. The next ten minutes was spent swaying around, giggling, trying to find everything. There is nothing better than a drunken giggle. Jeremy blamed the whole incident on me for being too drunk and completely overlooked his lack of driving skills whilst under the influence.

And so to bed for a few hours in order to get up to start all over again. There was only one house rule enforced by Belle, our hostess, and that was not to miss breakfast. Harsh, but fair. After all, you don't want your butler and chef hanging around doing nothing.

And when it's the chef's day off and you've got island fever, you simply book lunch in with a fellow millionaire on a neighbouring island.

* * * *

The fellow millionaire that Belle had booked lunch with was Ian Wace, hedge-fund manager. Ironically, he was suffering a little from island fever and was also dying to give his new speed-boat a run, so offered to come and collect us, just along the coast from the famous Basil's Bar. He and his model wife Saffron Aldridge cruised in, looking like characters from a James Bond movie, complete with a futuristic stealth-like, seemingly combat-ready speedboat.

We were whisked away to Canouan, another idyllic billionaires' playground, just five kilometres by five kilometres and, at that time, with hardly any inhabitants. We were driven through the huge hotel resort, which was in receivership or between owners so was like a luxury ghost town, with only a few staff polishing the silver and rolling up soft fluffy beach towels, as if expecting a plane full of holidaymakers. It was tragic to see, but we had a very special place to be, so headed on up into the hills eventually to arrive at yet another palatial holiday villa.

It was very much in keeping with the James Bond theme, set amongst beautifully landscaped gardens with a view to rival any other, looking out over St Vincent, the Grenadines and St Lucia. We were served cocktails and the obligatory face-freshening flannel, like any first-class hotel would provide. We were given the guided tour by Ian, the very proud owner, who loved and demonstrated the many gadgets that accessorised his holiday hideaway, including the vast array of electrically operated bespoke wooden blinds surrounding the main bedroom. Once open, they revealed another stunning panoramic view, framed by beautiful, colourful and fragrant tropical plants.

After our tour, and more cocktails, we were seated for lunch, another boozy long one with another token celebrity, hairdresser to the stars John Frieda (formerly married to Lulu) and his wife Avery Agnelli, widow of the Fiat heir Giovanni Agnelli. Ian wasn't drinking and was the perfect host. Saffron, on the other hand, loved a drink and ended up ramping the club music up and dancing on the table.

John, Avery and some of the other guests who were there to enjoy a yoga retreat retired to their rooms whilst, once

Saffron had calmed down, the rest of us had another laze around another luxury pool before making the hair-raising journey back to Mustique at high speed over quite a bumpy sea. Not such a treat, but you have to take the rough with the smooth, eh?

11

Around the World in Not Much More than Eighty Days

August 2013. In the few years up to this point, between all that I've shared here, we toured to St Petersburg, Moscow, Glasgow, Poland, South Africa and Australia with *Top Gear Live*. I had also nipped to the States a couple of times to take my son to visit his father. Jeremy was also filming all over the world and writing, while juggling life between London and Oxfordshire. We also had a couple of holidays with just the two of us, to the Seychelles, the south of France and Italy. From an idyllic spot on Lake Como, where I would have loved to have relaxed longer and for Jeremy to completely switch off, which he so very nearly had, we went to Mykonos. I think Jeremy actually regretted having accepted the invitation to Greece, to stay with Nick Allott and Christa D'Souza.

In true celebrity millionaire style, Jeremy had booked a private jet to get there. It was a real treat and I fully embraced the experience. I couldn't wait to crack open the champagne and quickly learnt that in a very small plane with the added pressure, champagne corks become lethal weapons, and so does alcohol. A small glass of the fizzy stuff went straight to my head and I became delirious with the giggles, which Jeremy found most amusing and said it was well worth the money to watch me lose control at several thousand feet.

Upon arrival at Nick and Christa's charming hillside Greek retreat, with its salt-water pool and jetty into the cool, calm waters of the Aegean Sea, one of the first conversations I had with Christa was about Nick and her concern that Jeremy would not have enough entertainment and partying whilst being tucked away in one of the quietest corners of the island. It started to worry me that the big man had a huge reputation as a party animal and was known for regularly being the last man standing. He seemed to have created a persona in his social circle that he felt he had to live up to, and that he should never be boring and say no to a night out or go home early. So, as he was staying out here, his friends thought that they must fuel that need. I could see he was beginning to be stuck in a bit of a vicious circle. It was becoming ridiculous.

I explained to Nick and Christa that actually Jeremy really needed a break and would be very happy to relax and enjoy leisurely lunches and dinners with just the four of us and their two boys. However, they did arrange lunch at one fellow islander's grand villa, complete with private beach, pool and even its own chapel.

So, off we went again for another lunch with people we didn't even know. It was really quite lovely despite Jeremy's fear that he had to perform as *The Jeremy Clarkson*, which of course he did, dutifully signing autographs and telling behind-the-scenes stories.

We all enjoyed the private beach with its selection of water toys and drinks from their own beach bar. The man of the house was a fascinating and incredibly clever man who designed and engineered factories in Africa. A core part of his business was to care for and develop local communities. All in all, not a bad day out with yet another multimillionaire. And I learnt about a new form of art: hyperrealism.

Our hosts had a Carole Feuerman sculpture, of a woman looking like she was leaning out of the swimming pool resting on a beach ball. It was freakily realistic, even down to the tone of her skin and the water droplets on it as well as her muscle structure and definition. A bit like a Madame Tussauds waxwork, I guess, but more refined. It was made out of some kind of resin and must be worth tens of thousands of pounds. I'm not sure if I like her work or not, but it is fascinating and I certainly appreciate it. You can Google her work, but to fully experience its 'is it real or not' element you need to see it up close and personal.

Imagine having enough money to be able to frivolously decorate the edge of your swimming pool at your holiday estate with valuable contemporary art. That is just one tiny example of the extraordinary world I had landed in.

That is something I really loved about my adventures with Mr Clarkson: the weird and wonderful things I got to see and experience and all the interesting characters. There were definitely a lot of bonuses to dating one of the most famous people in the UK and possibly the world. Jeremy is almost in the same league, excuse the pun, as Man United and Chelsea, or Coca-Cola. I was about to experience the downside to that fame.

12

One Step Too Far

So, after a relatively quiet week by Clarkson standards, it was decided that we should indulge in a bit of a party lunch at Mykonos's renowned party beach club, Nammos.

We joined a group of Nick and Christa's Mykonos friends at what is my idea of a nightmare, a beach full of sunbeds and parasols packed so tightly together you can't see the actual beach and a restaurant with tables squeezed in so tight you are literally climbing over people to get to your seat.

Bundle all that together with plenty of false boobs, teeth and hair on both males and females, with a soundtrack of club tracks played so loud you can't have a conversation, and I found myself feeling quite on edge. The only way I could deal with it was to get pissed and then it became good fun and the party posers dancing on the table were really quite entertaining.

Unfortunately, and it was to prove very unfortunate indeed, I was completely unaware of the prowling paparazzi lurking amongst the sun loungers and, true to form, the next day, Jeremy and I were all over the front pages of most newspapers, including shots of us canoodling – nobody wants to see that, do they? And least of all Jeremy's wife and children. Couple that with another story about his daughter hitting the press and you had a very explosive and panicky Clarkson. One that could not be calmed, or reasoned with.

Despite my offer to fly home with EasyJet while Jeremy stayed on our pre-booked BA flight, he was inconsolable and was convinced we'd be stalked by photographers all through the airports both in Greece and the UK. He couldn't face any more of it. I was instructed to book a private jet and in his blind panic he also insisted that it should be big enough for Nick and Christa and their son too, even though they, too, were happy to go home as planned on their discount airline.

The big man had spoken, so after many fraught phone calls, a jet was arranged. It's quite hard to suddenly arrange for the right-sized private plane and crew to arrive the next day on a Greek island with limited parking for non-scheduled aircraft. However, I'm not one to be defeated and failure is just not acceptable in Clarkson's World.

After a tense last evening, we all headed to the tiny airport where it soon became apparent that there was no private lounge, so the twenty-odd grand Jeremy had shelled out to protect his privacy was not really proving to be a good investment as we stood amongst all the other passengers waiting to board their reasonably priced flights.

Being quite used to these tricky situations, I soon arranged an alternative private waiting area in the back of an airport bus at the edge of the runway. At least Jeremy could easily step out for a fag. Ah, but he couldn't, not right next to a bunch of jets getting refuelled. It doesn't matter how famous you are, that is not allowed.

We waited and waited. I hardly dared to breathe the mood was so tense. After some more painful waiting and some desperate attempts to find out what was going on with our seemingly failed VIP travel, we finally had contact with the pilot, who told us that unfortunately, due to exceptionally strong headwinds, we would have to land in France to refuel, thereby extending our overall travel time to about seven hours.

Eek! No breathing, no talking, until the big man started to see the funny side of how shit VVIP travel can actually be, and began to warn our fellow travel companions that it would not be quite as luxurious as they might have imagined.

I don't know what Nick, Christa and their son had in mind, but the reality was that our private plane was private and had probably been private for many, many years. It looked worryingly tired and I'm not sure it had ever been luxury, even in its heyday.

As you know, Mr Clarkson is six-foot five-inches and Nick is over six foot too, with a decent width to match. Luckily, Christa is tiny and her son was still growing, so between us we managed to weave our limbs into the space provided to get reasonably comfy. And we hoped and prayed that none of us would need the loo because it wasn't much more than a 'bucket behind a curtain' at the back of the plane. The pilots simply turned around to make sure we were strapped in and off we set into the super-strong headwind.

Some time and a bumpy ride later, we touched down in a small airport in France, where we had to disembark while the pilots refuelled. Luckily, this tiny airport had a very pleasing lounge and bar area and we were the only customers. After a few drinks and a light snack, we felt it must be time to go.

Unfortunately not. It turned out that the pilot's payment card wasn't working and we were further delayed. This little treat of a 'luxury' flight home with no hassle was really not going terribly well. I think I'd stumbled upon a private plane company whose aircraft were held together with string, or so it seemed. Or perhaps a wing and a prayer!

Nearly nine hours later, we finally disembarked, somewhere in Hampshire. It was Farnborough probably, but I can't remember – must be my post-traumatic private-jet disorder. So only an hour or so back to London and job done. EasyJet, you have my heart and I shall never complain again about your shit food and long queues. The real kick in the teeth, or should I say in the boll**ks, for Jezza was that the guy who had arranged the plane for us didn't pay the company who had provided the plane and crew, so Jeremy was forced to pay many thousands again to avoid further legal dramas. That was a bad day in paradise.

* * * *

I dreaded airports with Jeremy. Unable to smoke, he became very tetchy and irritable and with the added angst of incoming fans at any minute he was very difficult to be around. Throw in the palaver of going through security and you find yourself with the worst travelling companion ever.

I eventually managed to persuade him to spend a bit more money – it might have been a few thousand pounds, but from the wallet of a millionaire that was just small change. It made such a difference to the holiday experience to book the private VIP service that most big international airports offer.

This was the ultimate stress-free way to fly. Your driver would drop you off right outside the door, where you would be greeted by pleasant and helpful staff who escorted you through to a lounge not dissimilar to your living room at home, with comfy sofa, tables and chairs, a decent-sized TV with remote control so you, rather than the airport manager, decided what you watched.

Food and drink was served on request and you were even given a personal shopper who would go into the duty-free shops on your behalf to fill your order of booze, fags, perfume – whatever you wanted. For chain-smoking Mr Clarkson, he could even nip outside for a cheeky fag.

When it was time to fly, you went through a small private security and scanning area and were then driven out to the plane as close to take-off time as possible. Why wouldn't you? If you weren't a pennies-conscious Yorkshireman! We only did it a couple of times, much to my frustration.

I was desperate to have a simple holiday with just the two of us, or with the kids, for a bit of normality and some quality downtime. We did manage a couple of low-key trips. My favourite of all was after Jeremy had been away with A A Gill to write a joint piece for *The Times*. They made the front cover of *The Sunday Times Magazine*. It's a wonderful photo of them both looking truly happy. The piece was based around the fact that Jeremy loved the French while Adrian despised them.

The two very opinionated good friends and equally offensive journalists have written a few features together like this. They are well worth a read to enjoy the friendly but sometimes very pointed abuse they direct at each other. There's a classic quote from Adrian in this particular piece about Jeremy not being recognised – not terribly offensive, but funny: 'A Frenchman spots Jeremy – "Eet is Tom Jones".'

Jeremy obviously *was* truly happy, as his trip with Adrian inspired him to want to take me for a few quiet days in France, to repeat the tranquillity he had enjoyed on a canal-boat trip down the Canal du Midi in the south of France. One of the reasons Jeremy loves France is because he is not recognised very often, by the French at least. They may think he's Tom Jones, but then they don't shout any abuse, I assume, because Sir Tom never offended anyone, did he?

The trip was so wonderfully basic and peaceful, in stark contrast to our luxury star-studded escapes to Mustique and the like. We had a blissful few days cruising through the picturesque south of France, mooring up for a boozy lunch with no concerns about drink-driving or being hassled for selfies. On the odd occasion Jeremy was spotted by fellow Englishmen, we were on our boat and just floated away. You can't just suddenly turn around and put your foot down in a canal boat. As Jeremy had discovered, you were forced into a slower pace of life and he actually loved it. I even persuaded the big man to get on his bike and we had a hilarious bike ride into one of the nearby villages.

The only other strenuous activity was navigating the locks. The only pressure was making sure you got through them before they closed. Who'd have thought Clarkson Almighty would be as happy as Captain Pugwash on a calm sea squashed into a plastic canal boat with no luxury trimmings or fine dining, just good old bread, cheese and wine. Always the wine.

Another last-minute escape to a more ordinary destination available to the 'common people' was a birthday treat for me (although I organised and paid for it), a classic city break to Barcelona. Jeremy had suggested the Arts Hotel, close to the beach, which was amazing. We had a stunning corner suite with floor-to-ceiling glass offering panoramic views of the ocean, city and the hills beyond.

The downside to being in a hotel in a bustling European city is that Jeremy was bound to be recognised. Constantly being recognised was a big part of Jeremy's life in the spotlight, or should I say headlights. The irony of having a lot of money and the social standing that sees you being invited everywhere and having the ability to go wherever you like was being essentially trapped in your own luxury prison.

*　*　*　*

Back in London, Jeremy constantly sent me out for fags, food, newspapers and booze, even for just a quick trip across the road from his flat in London, as he couldn't bear being yelled at by passing cabbies and lorry drivers or being surrounded by schoolchildren begging for autographs and selfies.

Of course that didn't happen every minute of every trip, but he couldn't bear the thought of it and spent a lot of time imprisoned in his Holland Park penthouse flat. It was especially bad after any controversy, of which there were quite a few.

In the aftermath of 'that punch', although there was a back door to the block of flats, which, in theory, was on private land behind electric gates, it didn't stop the ferociously persistent paps. We once came home from a party, weirdly and I don't know why, with Rachel Johnson, broadcaster and journalist and, of course, Boris's sister. We arrived back at the flat in an executive car with a driver who we were used to and who knew us. We used to call him Mark Strong because that is exactly who he looked like, and was even built like. On this occasion, he turned into a potential Mark Strong movie character. He had to double as a bodyguard.

He drove us right around the back of the property, out of sight of the long lenses. However, one rogue paparazzo must have snuck through the gates behind the car, aiming and firing his long lens and flash. It literally did feel like coming under fire, a very strange experience that made you panic – I don't know why because what's the worst they can do? Get a dreadful shot of you with a ridiculous face?

I didn't really care. The big man, however, hated it and had explained to me that what it means to him is that his face will be all over the world again repeating the news of his latest controversy. Admittedly, his bad behaviour surrounding 'the punch' was not acceptable and a lot of the incidents in his life did not play out in the media, but for newspapers and magazines to keep going over the same old ground, sometimes making assumptions about what he had done, was unnecessary. What I found puzzling, though, about Jeremy's personality and that of others like him is the love-hate relationship with the attention fame brings.

I've had my fair share of paparazzi chases, including one whilst I was leaving the flat one day. There was an army of them, literally creating a blockade in front of the gates. In my panic, I forgot which way the electric gates opened and got the front of my car stuck on them, at which point a determined pap opened the boot of my car to try to get his shot. What the fu**? He must have jumped over the wall. To be fair to the others, they did concede and I think felt sorry for me as I tried to remove my car from the gates. I heard one of them say, 'Let her out,' and I was free to speed off down the road.

It's a very strange thing being super-famous and especially for someone like Jeremy, who courts controversy – it's very much part of his brand. The trouble is, you can't switch fame off. You have to be a very grounded, strong person to put yourself out there and keep putting yourself out there to sustain your high profile and career. Jeremy had a choice to move over to the slow lane, but I think he had a real need for speed. An addiction almost.

When in a hotel, we more often than not had breakfast in our room, or as in this case, our suite, which of course was no hardship, except that you never got a decent cup of tea or coffee as it had always travelled miles through endless hotel corridors and lifts. When you're wealthy, you are usually on the top floor, miles from the kitchen. Although in really posh hotels there are often separate service facilities, like laundries, housekeeping and kitchens set up close to the most expensive and exclusive rooms and suites in order to provide an express, first-class service. In really top suites, you have your own kitchen with butler, too; you call him when required and he magically appears. Alternatively, you can brew your own cuppa, which, let's face it, is often the best way to get exactly what you want.

Inevitably, as we ventured out into the common areas of our swanky Barcelona hotel, Jeremy was recognised. The hotel was super-busy and the big man complained, suggesting it was full of businessmen at a conference or on a team-building weekend. How wrong he was. The next thing we knew we had come face to face with Adrian Newey, the master of F1 engineering. It was pre-season testing for all the F1 teams at the Circuit de Barcelona-Catalunya.

Adrian very kindly invited us out to the circuit to watch and mingle with the teams. Any other time, I would have jumped at the chance, but right then I thought, noooo, please just let us have quiet couple time, a weekend with just us. Luckily Jeremy felt the same way and we headed off to explore Barcelona.

As with most of our trips, it wasn't all plain sailing. We did manage to meander down Las Ramblas and get lost in the labyrinth of the Gothic Quarter, but finding the Gaudi's famous unfinished Sagrada Família cathedral required a seemingly unending walk, which was not pleasing to his lordship. By the time we finally reached it, he was in no mood to face the crowds of tourists, most of whom were Chinese and not interested in him, but unfortunately, when Jeremy sees a crowd, especially one armed with cameras, it triggers him to want to make a sharp exit. So, my long-awaited visit to one of the most famous cathedrals, one which is truly unique, was left unfinished too.

13

'Clarkson – available for children's parties, weddings, bar mitzvahs ... ?'

Back in the UK, our mad social life continued, with more wonderful weekends at Jemima's, evenings at Eric Fellner's film club at Working Title and sometimes we would go to other private screenings or other friends' private cinemas, like Matthew Freud's. Matthew's personal movie theatre, like Jemima Khan's, was in a separate building to the main house and was the biggest private home cinema I had seen amongst Jeremy's super-wealthy friends. Matthew's cinema had a kitchen to the side of it which was stocked with drinks and sweet machines to stock up from, just as you would in a public cinema. I have a feeling we went there to watch a big rugby game and Matthew had his staff provide a buffet of burgers and hot dogs with all the trimmings.

Jeremy loves film, and perhaps once a week, usually the night before recording *Top Gear* down at the track, we would actually stay in and watch the latest offering on Netflix, and lately Amazon too, of course. I remember when Jeremy first got Amazon installed at the flat in London, we had spent some time revamping the place as he was spending more and more time there and the farm wasn't habitable yet. The most important upgrade was the living room. Inspired by a living room that Jeremy was filming in for an Amazon advert, the whole room was redesigned around a huge cinema-style screen and surrounding cabinet. Watching films was Jeremy's main hobby, alongside partying.

A perfect couple to combine the two activities, Claudia Winkleman and Kris Thykier, invited us to the preview of Kris's latest film, *Summer of '92*, a wonderful true story about the Danish national football team beating Germany. Kris is part Danish. It's a real feel-good film about a team which was originally knocked out, but got invited back in to the tournament when Yugoslavia were forced to pull out due to civil war breaking out. With only a week to train, the Danish team manager Richard Nielsen pulls together his unfit, mismatched team of national superstars and nobodies to take the title. Against all odds, the great Danes went on to win the European Championships.

I highly recommend it if you can get hold of it. I think it only made it big in Denmark, perhaps unsurprisingly, and I'm sure you won't find it on a DVD rack in Germany! And here is another six degrees of separation about the lovely couple: Claudia is the daughter of Eve Pollard, now Lady Lloyd, who has been editor for various tabloids including the *News of the World*, which provides the link to Rebekah Brooks, who is Matthew Freud's neighbour in Oxfordshire; and Matthew is a very close friend and business partner of Kris. Matthew Freud was married to Liz Murdoch of the notorious Murdoch empire; Claudia is very good friends with Victoria Coren Mitchell, sister of Giles Coren, another journalist and broadcaster who has worked for *The Times* for many years, as does Jeremy and as did Adrian Gill. Giles Coren's wife is the sister of Alexander Armstrong's wife and they both live in the neighbourhood of Jeremy, Rebekah and Charlie, Matthew and Liz – keeping up? I never could and, in fact, I may have got some of the connections slightly wrong, but they definitely *are* all connected! And now I was an honorary member of this bizarre club.

* * * *

Talking of Matthew Freud reminds me of two weird and wonderful social gatherings we had with him. Perhaps the most odd was when Jeremy was invited to attend his son's birthday, his tenth, I think. I couldn't quite believe that Jeremy had agreed to go, considering how little time he had to see his own family and to do what he actually wanted to do. However, he'd said yes to Matthew and he is not one for letting anyone down once he's committed.

We drove out to Burford Priory, a good hour's drive from London. It's a stunning Grade I listed manor in one of the most picturesque parts of the Cotswolds. So picturesque, unfortunately, that right outside the front gates of this beautiful residence is a coach park, where all the tourist coaches park, whilst hundreds of excited sightseers gaze at the beautifully unspoilt town, preserved in its centuries-old glory. It is often referred to as the Gateway to the Cotswolds.

And here's my six degrees of separation: it turns out that one of my closest friends in Hertfordshire is actually related to some of the original owners of Burford Priory. Those friends were actually embraced into Jeremy's world, maybe because of their heritage – who knows? – but they could also shoot, which is one of Jeremy's few hobbies, so that may have favoured them too. They were the only friends of mine who were actually invited out to the farm at Chadlington.

Anyway, back to the birthday party. As we drove up in a Ferrari no less (also requested by Matthew), Jeremy explained to me that it was important to have Matthew on side as he ran a large PR company which wielded significant power over the press, which might be very useful should Jeremy ever need a story kept out of the papers. This service was of course quite likely to be needed given Jeremy's track record. Okay, fair enough, I thought, but to have to turn up essentially as the children's entertainer was, I felt, a step too far.

On the plus side, it was a beautiful day and I always enjoy kids' company. They didn't disappoint. I found it fascinating that young children enjoyed watching *Top Gear*, which, let's face it, was all about three old men making fools of themselves with cars. I wondered how the younger generation related to a generation so far from theirs. I asked a group of them how old they thought Jeremy was. They replied, 'Thirty … thirty-five?' That, I think, proves just how powerful having a childish attitude can help in keeping you young, or, should I say, in giving you the illusion of youth.

I have to admit that, despite my reservations as to why we were wasting valuable time entertaining someone else's kids, it was fun playing with a Ferrari, some rage buggies, a lake and a swimming pool and having a delicious lunch with Princess Diana's brother's wife (she was formerly Matthew's wife) in the beautiful garden of a Cotswolds manor house. I couldn't really complain. It gets more and more Jilly Cooper by the minute, doesn't it!?

* * * *

Ooh, I've just thought of a third social encounter that perhaps tops them all, but more about that later. In the meantime, the more grown-up event we went to was back in London at the GQ Awards after-show party. Matthew's brother, Tom, put on the show. Tom runs an events company that is renowned for showstopping parties, including Mr Clarkson's own fiftieth.

Somewhere in deepest, darkest London, Tom took over a stunning house; in fact, it may well have been Liz and Matthew's London residence. It was another film set of a venue, with a gated courtyard entrance similar to Jemima Khan's. It was heavily guarded by burly security men on this occasion. In the courtyard was a cool burger van dishing out late-night snacks to help soak up the alcohol that had already been consumed at the award ceremony.

Just opposite the burger bar was a specially built wine cellar, which I remember sniffing around with JC, who is obviously a big fan of fine wines. My first celebrity spot was a big one: Samuel L Jackson, who was chatting to Jeremy's nemesis, Piers Morgan. I tried to steer Jeremy away from them as I was genuinely nervous of something kicking off between them. (For those of you who don't know, Jeremy and Piers have actually had a fight. Jeremy famously punched Piers at another awards dinner some years before and they continued to battle it out by way of Twitter social-media tittle-tattle and in their newspaper columns. There is definitely no love lost between them.) Jeremy insisted on saying hello – I can't remember his exact words – but they both said something derogatory about each other, like sparring teenagers in the playground.

Moving quickly on to the bar, we found Russell Brand, who was flirting with Jemima Khan, with whom he later went on to have a relationship. I found Russell charming, and he was really kind to me after putting his foot in it, referring to Jeremy's 'other women' being all over the newspapers. I think Jeremy had recently been papped with some glamorous women on a night out, which, at the time, although I was told it was innocent, was still upsetting. Russell kept apologising and checking up on me throughout the evening; he also cheered me up with his ridiculous humour. I like Russell; Jeremy is not a fan. Jeremy is actually not too dissimilar from Russell: very clever, a bit naughty, expert at spreading his strong opinions where they might not be wanted, and definitely never far from a good-looking woman.

Jeremy has been splashed over the newspapers with, among others: Miss Iceland, 'a good friend of his', who he has been seen falling out of a nightclub with; Jemima Khan (they were regularly plus-ones for one another); the TV producer Elaine Bedell, with whom he got caught in several suspicious clinches; ex-model Gabriela Peacock, with whom he had regular lunches, along with other high-society ladies who lunch, including Princess Beatrice; Charlotte Edwardes, another former model; Martha Ward, fashion PR guru; Lily Fortescue, underwear entrepreneur – whatever that means; and Sophie Stanbury, reality TV star. I could go on, but it could get boring. Jezza was definitely a man about town.

The GQ party was a strange environment, with wall-to-wall celebrities, the majority of whom knew Jeremy, of course. Many conversations were struck up as if they were long-lost friends, with the likes of Noel Gallagher from Oasis and Matt Smith of *Doctor Who* and *The Crown* fame, Rob Brydon, comedian, actor and presenter, The Arctic Monkeys and so many more it was just a blur, but not half as blurry as the evening looked for our host Tom, who, at the end of the evening, as we sat in the seventies-style living room next door to the glass-encased swimming pool, just passed out, absolutely off his face on God knows what. Or maybe he was just exhausted? A pure party pro.

To give Tom Freud his due, he does pull off a good party, especially when given a huge budget to work with. Jeremy's fiftieth was no exception. A huge marquee 'village' was erected and a dance-floor built over the swimming pool at Jeremy's family home in the Cotswolds.

We were greeted by golf buggies to take us from the parking in the paddocks up to the house, where canapés and champagne were served by an army of staff in the courtyard garden. A chosen few of the crew from *Top Gear Live* and the BBC programme were there and were staying in a hotel down the road, where I and my plus-one were. I became very over-excited meeting up with everyone from our touring days and was also just a tad nervous as 'the mistress'. Forever playful, I was standing up on the back of a golf buggy cheering on a race with Tiff Needell's buggy. Probably not the best way to enter a party when you're the 'other woman'.

After downing a few glasses of bubbles and a bit of celeb-spotting, we were led through the conservatory into a marquee tunnel leading through to the huge dining area, where we were wined, dined and entertained. Each table was beautifully dressed and there were party giveaways of mugs and ashtrays with 'I've been to Jeremy Clarkson's 50th Birthday Party and all I got was this' painted on them.

With the help of some special friends, a film montage of birthday wishes from some of the guests who couldn't be there and others who just wanted to perform was shown on a huge screen. The then prime minister David Cameron performed in a skit from his office, Jimmy Carr had staged and filmed a spoof scene in bed with Jeremy's wife and my favourite was Will Young singing Jeremy a love song whilst in his underpants – I don't know why, but it was very funny. (They weren't Jeremy's underpants, by the way. That really would have been weird.)

There was no expense spared, as you might imagine. Jeremy had his favourite band Squeeze playing and The Who's Roger Daltrey. The birthday boy was surprised by his family with a West Highland Terrier puppy, which was presented to him on stage. The big surprise for me was that while I knew Jeremy loves Motown, as I do, I'd never pictured him swirling around the dance-floor to The Supremes and Michael Jackson. The DJ rolled out a load of those sixties classics. It was all going on, my friend SJ and I were shaking our stuff with TV presenters Adrian Chiles and Patrick Kielty and my favourite, Alex James, from Blur, now known for his cheese-making on his neighbouring Cotswolds farm. I complimented him by saying, 'You're so happy!' as he threw some moves on the dance-floor with a permanent grin on his face, alone in the dance-crazed crowd. As I've said before, I was so naive. I now know that Alex is absolutely no stranger to party treats, and I strongly suspect he'd had a few.

There was a cocktail bar and a constant supply of food and drink rolling out from the caterer's marquee, including a huge tableful of bowls of sweets at the end of the evening for late-night munchies.

The usual suspects of the Chipping Norton Set were there, along with Dom Joly, Jodie Kidd, Steve Coogan, Jimmy Carr, Sir Tim Rice, Anneka Rice, Vicki Butler-Henderson and her lovely husband Phil, who was the main *Top Gear* director and went on to *The Grand Tour*. Andy Wilman, Jeremy's childhood friend and *Top Gear* and *The Grand Tour*'s producer was there and, of course, Richard Hammond and Mindy, and James May and his partner, Sarah, a dance critic.

It was a night that didn't really end but rolled on to breakfast and a hangover lunch for those who crashed at Clarkson Towers and the locals. Clarkson apparently fell asleep on the sofa and woke up next to Jodie Kidd.

The rest of us carried on in our hotel bar. I didn't make breakfast or lunch, despite Jeremy begging me to go. I thought that was pushing it too far, and very unfair to be at the family house as the 'other woman'.

14

Phillipa Jane, Meet Tarzan

Back to our life when we were out and about as an official couple. We had a never-ending whirlwind of nights out, with a constant stream of major and minor celebs. We were regulars at Jemima's wonderful Kiddington Estate and I continued to enjoy the company of fascinating fellow guests like Kate Reardon, then the editor of *Tatler* and a fellow keen horsewoman. Perhaps the most interesting guest of all was Ralph Bousfield who was with Caro Hickman, former wife of Steve Coogan and a very good friend of Jemima.

Ralph is a real-life Tarzan, he even sported long hair, topping his toned and jungle-scarred body. He runs exclusive safari holidays at Jack's Camp in Botswana in the Makgadikgadi Salt Pans, where *Top Gear* filmed one of their epic adventures, which I believe was inspired by a Clarkson family holiday hosted by Ralph. Jeremy often used his personal holidays as recces for *Top Gear* films.

Ralph was born in Tanzania, where his father, Jack, was a hunter and they lived as a bush family – a totally feral life. Jack had a copy of Livingstone's map. After studying it, he decided to retrace Livingstone's steps across the Kalahari Desert and set up the first photographic safari camp where they lived among San people, whose ancestors had survived there for thousands of years.

Jack was known for his prolific hunting; he earned a Guinness World Record for shooting over 53,000 crocodiles. But he was a pioneer in changing safaris from trophy-hunting holidays to photographic safaris as he learned to conserve the environment and its glorious wildlife.

When Jack tragically died in a plane crash, it was entirely natural for Ralph to take over from where his father had left off. He has created a stunning base, with luxurious safari tents, with sumptuous interiors, decorated with antiques, creating a glamorous forties feel with no lack of comfort despite being in the middle of the desert amongst mighty lions and cheeky meerkats.

You don't meet many men like Ralph. I felt very honoured to have met him. He has done his extraordinary father proud, continuing his legacy of working, learning and educating others alongside the San people and the extraordinary wildlife of this very special and magical place. Jack's Camp is definitely on my bucket list.

I do not know how on earth I fitted in, little old me, Jeremy Clarkson's Girlfriend, which felt like my only title and achievement. I guess the fact that I was genuinely interested in what everyone did and how they were, went a long way. Everyone else was 'somebody' and at the top of their game, including one of Jemima's boyfriends, another gentle and very talented soul, John Battsek, producer of some truly outstanding documentaries, such as *Searching for Sugar Man*, *Mystify*, about the life of Michael Hutchence, and *The Imposter*, which Jeremy and I went to see at Channel 4 in a small screening room, before discussing it over dinner. It was such a privilege to be amongst all these great people and it turned out I managed to fit in very well.

* * * *

I was becoming more and more comfortable with this extraordinary lifestyle, so was totally unfazed when Jeremy announced that Sir/Lord Andrew and Madeleine Lloyd-Webber had invited us to their home in Barbados, but more about that later.

By this time, we had had successful holidays in the south of France with Jeremy's children, although there was always a drama of some kind, often caused by the big man's overindulgence in alcohol and other party habits, but the good outweighed the bad. We had a big road trip, *Top Gear*-style from Siena, in Italy, to St Tropez, in the south of France. We never fell out on a road trip; we both loved the adventure of travel. I found it both extraordinary and endearing that Jeremy, who must be one of the world's most well-travelled men, never tired of travel.

The previous week, I'd been out in Tuscany with Jeremy and Richard Hammond filming for their annual DVD. I went from following JC through the stunning Tuscan scenery in a gull-winged supercar and being track-side at the Mugello Circuit, to flying home to take my boy and my parents to Scotland in a camper-van (never again!). From there it was back out to Italy to attend the famous Palio in Siena as special guests of the mayor, which had been organised by Brian Klein, a *Top Gear* director, who also directed Jeremy's DVDs.

As guests of the mayor, we were in the best seats in the house overlooking the racetrack, which was set up in the main square. We were actually in the mayor's office, or town hall as we would call it. It was a stunning building in which, as usual when with Jeremy, we were given VIP treatment and allowed up to an exclusive terrace that looked over the Tuscan hills beyond the city. Another film-set moment.

As a horse lover, I was not too keen on the race itself. It has a horrible history of both horses and riders dying. I feel the same about the Grand National; the jockeys know the risk they are taking, but the horses don't, and I don't like what they have to endure while a load of people are screaming at them because they want to win a few quid.

However, like the Grand National, the Palio has cleaned up its act a little. The number of horses racing has been reduced from seventeen to ten and the surface has been improved, with more earth being laid down over the hard cobbles to create the track around the edge of the square.

Each horse represents a different *contrada*, a region within the city. Each *contrada* has their own colours in different flag designs, which all their supporters carry and wave frantically. So that each *contrada* has a chance to enter their horse in the race, the Palio is now run twice a year.

It's an extraordinary event that has taken place since medieval times; and it maintains a medieval feel, with thousands of locals and tourists from around the world showing up to watch.

I have to say, although I was a little apprehensive about it as I did not want to witness any cruelty to the horses or see any horrific accidents, I loved it. It was like being taken back in time. The square is surrounded by buildings dating right back to the sixteenth century, and even before then, and on Palio day it looks and feels medieval.

There is an amazing pageant, with a cast of hundreds dressed in really authentic costumes, fit for any Hollywood blockbuster's wardrobe department. It was indeed a performance. There was a parade of floats drawn by huge oxen, larger than any

I'd ever seen before. They stood at least six feet high and were about eight feet long from nose to tail. The floats carried trumpeters and dignitaries. Each person in the pageant was in full theatrical costume, including wigs and boots specially made for the occasion.

Even the buildings were dressed up, with flags and drapes hanging out of the windows and over balconies. It really could have been a film set, and indeed has been, for the Bond film *Quantum of Solace*.

My concerns about the horses diminished as we got up close and personal with the animal VIPs of the day, who waited in special, grand stables in the lower part of the town hall. They were in peak condition and were clearly cherished by their grooms and jockeys.

The medieval way of racing was maintained in the way the race was started. Two ropes contain all the runners, behind and in front. Nine of the ten horses line up in an order determined by lots being drawn. The tenth horse is kept out and its handlers think tactically about where to enter, watching the others for bad behaviour which may cause them to start badly. Once the tenth horse has entered the roped-off area, the starter drops the front rope.

The starting procedure can take a while, which increases the tension. The atmosphere is electric and reaches a spectacular crescendo when the race finally gets going. It is absolutely insane. The jockeys ride bareback and I have never seen horses run so fast around such a tight circuit. Some jockeys don't make it and fly off, often in the corners. They are like acrobats, though, and roll and tumble their way out of danger.

The incredibly fast race is over in about ninety seconds after three laps of the circuit. A horse can win without its jockey; it is the horse that is the hero, jockey or no jockey, and the winner is proudly paraded around the circuit on a lap of honour by a crowd of people from its *contrada*. It's a pretty extreme sport, but an incredible spectacle to watch, and the celebrations go on long into the night.

We, however, headed on to join Nicola Formby and Adrian Gill at the village where Domitilla Harding, née Getty (as in the notorious Getty billionaire family), lives in the stunning hills close to Siena. Just a slight contrast to my night in a campervan in a pub car park overlooking Hadrian's Wall.

The village is utterly, magically charming. Domi, as she's known, is a designer of furniture and clothing – she is the designer behind the Miss Italy label. She's also a very successful glass sculptor, who has had her work shown in various museums and galleries all over the world.

Domi is also a generous hostess, who made us feel very welcome in her one-of-a-kind home. She has transformed a tumbledown village into her own private resort, creating guest suites out of the original hillside cottages and barns. It was genius. We were given two cottages which were linked together at the northern end of the village. To go to dinner, we left the rustic comfort of our cottage suite to walk through the village square, complete with water feature, to join the rest of the guests in the dining cottage, which had an outdoor, covered lounge/bar area in which to relax after dinner. The only downside was that we were only there for two nights before it was time to speed off to St Tropez.

* * * *

And speed we had to in order to attend another party-of-the-century aboard the Dunstones' recently launched super-luxury superyacht. I'm not sure if technically it was classed as a superyacht, but it definitely was super. Don't think Russian oligarch, think thirties socialite.

Of course, we had the right car for the job. One of the perks of being Jeremy Clarkson is you can ask your PA to speak to the motor manufacturer of your choice and demand the car you've chosen to be delivered to the airport you nominate. I think in this instance it was a Jaguar, a supercharged one, but one that could accommodate all the kids too; whereas when we were touring around Lake Como we had the latest Jaguar F-type convertible, which had my favourite ridiculous gadget: a noise button that you could press to get that real hearty gurgle through the mountain tunnels – great fun, if very childish.

After an incredibly long drive, with a short pit stop to pick up my boy and his carer (and my friend) from the airport, we arrived at our villa, which came with its own housekeeping staff and chef. There was no time to settle in; there was a party to get to.

After a quick shower, we were off to the port to be met by the Dunstones' tender, the small boat used to transfer passengers to and from yachts that are too big to come right in to port. Strangely, I was no stranger to this rather unusual way of arriving at a party. Whilst touring in Australia with *Top Gear Live* we commandeered a superyacht to take the three boys to and from the venue they were performing at and we used it for entertaining, too, but our parties on tour were, as you might imagine, quite casual affairs. Here in St Tropez, heading to a high-society do, I was in a long dress and heels, which does not make climbing on and off a dinghy-type vessel that's bobbing up and down on the sea very easy, nor is it very kind to your hair. However, I kept my cool whilst boarding the most beautiful yacht I'd ever seen.

Charles Dunstone, a keen seaman, had fallen in love with the thirties-built 64.4-metre *Shemara* in the mid-2000s and had eventually persuaded her then owner to sell her to him several years later. With his entrepreneurial drive, he set up his own boat-refit company and spent the next few years and hundreds of thousands of pounds creating a mini *Titanic*.

Once again, I felt like I had landed on a film set. *Shemara* is absolutely stunning. The immaculate decks of polished wood and brass, lit up by white lights strung all around, looked every inch as good as, if not way better than, she must have looked in her original glory days.

She set the perfect St Tropez scene for all the glamorous guests being served by crew, dressed all in white, who wove unobtrusively amongst us with champagne and canapés. I loved the decks, but even the funnels and masts had a romance and elegance about them. The original Hollywood-style thirties elegance was maintained with wicker chairs and highly polished solid wood tables. The beautiful fitted solid wood curved benches following the lines of the boat were softened with plenty of cushions.

The upper deck had a more modern twist, with the look of an Ibiza beach club lounge. There were huge deck cushions and bright orange scatter cushions to lie on and decadently sip champagne under the Mediterranean sky.

The boat's interior took your breath away; think Ritz Hotel meets *Titanic* in Soho House. It was as if you had been magically transported and were now in a palatial seven-star hotel suite, complete with huge marble fireplace surrounded by sumptuous sofas. There was another huge dining table dressed with grand silver candelabras.

It was easy to forget you were on a boat, but the portholes kept reminding you. There was a bar where Sir Charles would not have been out of place in a velvet smoking jacket, lounging on the bespoke leather Chesterfield, supping a martini whilst waiting for dinner to be served. I cannot do it justice in words; you must Google *Shemara*.

The party partied on and the tender was busy till the early hours of the morning. Jeremy managed to shake off his tiredness from our epic drive from Italy and was very happy amongst what appeared to be the entire Chipping Norton Set *en Français*. I had another bizarre six-degrees-of-separation moment as I met an old school friend-of-a-friend who I used to live with in Knebworth, Hertfordshire. This was Charlie Pragnell of Pragnell jewellers. Charlie commented on my necklace, which I had designed and had made up by Byworth jewellers. We were all connected. It is truly a very small world in a very strange way.

Meanwhile, Jeremy had secured invitations to parties at the Gallaghers' villa, which dominated one corner of St Tropez, an inland gig at Alex James's and back-to-back lunches and dinners. I longed for a holiday!

We had several lunches and dinners, many of which were at the famous beachside restaurant Le Club 55, where we dined alongside Joan Collins, Elton John and a good smattering of models, actors and the super-rich. It gets absolutely packed in the summer and almost unbearable in the heat; to save the day and keep the punters coming they have created a unique sprinkler system to cool you as you dine. They are famous for giant bowls – so big, they call them boats – of crudités, providing enough fresh veg to feed a small village with their five a day.

You knew you'd arrived somewhere special at Le Club 55 when you were trying to find a parking space amongst the dozens of Porsches, Ferraris, Bentleys and the like. The car park was actually like a supercar showroom.

For extra holiday entertainment, Jeremy chartered a boat, much smaller than the Dunstones' mighty launch, but one that could accommodate the two of us, his three children and their friends, my boy and Corrina, his carer, and a crate of rosé. Off we went for snorkelling and silly sea activities like strapping on some boots and getting fired up into the air by an extremely powerful jet of water. Not for me, thanks, nor for the big man.

Family time was spent in the town square playing boules in the shade of the plane trees and alongside a local superstar, David Ginola, ex-Newcastle and Spurs footballer and model for L'Oréal hair products – because 'he was worth it'. Another little moment of six degrees of separation: I used to work for a football agent in my late teens and early twenties and had socialised with David, enjoying an epic night out in Newcastle with fellow Toon Army and England stars Les Ferdinand and Warren Barton. But that's another story.

* * * *

The next holiday highlight was to blow the small party on the Dunstones' luxury yacht out of the water. We had been invited to the Bamfords' château and, more importantly for Jeremy, the vineyard of Mr Bamford's best friend, Daylesford's organic Château Léoube Rosé.

To get there, we chartered another boat and set off around the coast looking for the Bamfords' yacht – that was the 'seamark', shall we say, to indicate we were in the right spot to be transported to the château. There were a few 'is that it?' moments before, 'No, that's it!' as a yacht not at all dissimilar from the *Royal Yacht Britannia* was spotted floating majestically in a bay.

We then, for some complicated nautical reason, had to moor our teeny-tiny boat alongside and climb, way too high for my liking, aboard yet another incredible vessel, aided by the royal-looking, smartly uniformed crew, who then helped us to board their very smart tender to take us to the beach and a small house beyond, nestled in the rocks and shrub. That four-bedroom-sized house was actually just a gatehouse where we were met by yet more staff, who drove us for about a mile up a dirt track to arrive at yet another film set, this time a Disney one.

The château was perfectly formed, with four turrets, adorned with powder-blue shutters and surrounded by lavender, roses and Mediterranean herbs. It was out of this world. It looked every inch like a Disney princess's abode. Everything was beautiful and immaculate. The gardens had been landscaped, creating terraces which descended towards the sea, from the herb gardens to the pool area, to formal lawn areas, to the vineyards and to paddocks where fairy-tale Camargue white horses topped off the surreal scene.

We had another endless lunch, fuelled by gallons of rosé and, when we were able to move again, we were given a guided tour of the vineyard and the huge ten-foot wooden barrels in the bespoke wine cellar. I have pictures of the big man praying to these and getting on his hands and knees to drink straight from the tap. I, also a bit drunk, climbed on top of one and straddled it as if it were a horse.

I had a tour with Lady Bamford and a few of the other guests of the whole château, which truly was of fairy-tale or royal standard. What was lovely to see was Carole's – Lady Bamford's – pride and love for the place and how she wished her mother was still alive for her to share it with. The Bamfords are incredibly wealthy, but amazingly grounded and very generous. They made my boy very welcome. I think he thought he'd died and gone to heaven, having a pool to himself and a cinema room just across the terrace with food and drink on tap.

Rosé ordered and ready for shipment back to the UK, it was time to head back to our humble chartered boat, which, thank the Lord, came with a captain, since nobody in our party was fit to navigate us back to St Tropez.

It had been a holiday of much extravagance, creating many memories, both good and bad. My favourite moment came when my son, a boy of few words (he's autistic) said to me, 'The chef is cooking my pasta.' I was so proud that he'd strung together a whole sentence, but I prayed he wasn't going to repeat it back at school, where most of the children's summer treats would have been a trip to McDonald's.

15

Wham! Bam! You Are My Man

Just to recap, in this year alone, since January, we had been on tour with *Top Gear Live* in Scotland, Russia, South Africa, Italy, Croatia, Hungary and the Czech Republic. We'd been filming in Morocco and Tuscany, then managed to squeeze in holidays in the States, Scotland, Devon, Mustique and the south of France. And it wasn't over yet.

Jeremy would have travelled even more than that, filming for BBC *Top Gear*, and obviously there were parties, too. We had Chris Hughes, *Top Gear Live*'s tour manager's fiftieth, which was really messy. Jeremy and I started off drinking in the bar of our hotel, with the Pied Piper of drinking Chris Evans and his lovely wife Tash. That became slightly uncomfortable as the two big egos started a heated debate. Tash and I rolled our eyes and decided it was time to get a taxi to the party.

Chris, not known for small celebrations, had gone all out and hired a huge warehouse which his event company team had themed and dressed. We entered via a marquee which led to a series of screened-off areas set up like airport security, where we were frisked and searched by Chris himself and members of the *Top Gear Live* tour crew dressed as security men and women, who got well into character, demanding we take shoes off etc. Airport security was one of Chris's pet hates and Jeremy's too; I think the whole over-the-top gag was aimed at him. Chris always liked to entertain and to keep Jeremy happy in order to keep rolling him out across the world delivering live shows to thousands of eager fans, making thousands of pounds to help pay for silly over-the-top parties like this one. To give him his due, Chris knew how to throw a good party.

After a champagne reception and a speech from the birthday boy, we were led through a small, Narnia-style 'forest' which opened out into a funfair complete with full-size dodgems. Mixing alcohol with the celebrity egos of Clarkson and Evans battling it out with Hammond, May and The Stig in bumper cars was a terrifying spectacle. The birthday boy had to deflate all egos when one of them threw a traffic cone. Do not try this at home is all I can say.

We were fed by celebrity chef Tom Kerridge and entertained by the Kaiser Chiefs and our favourite karaoke band Rockaoke and numerous members of Chris's incredibly talented family. There was the traditional band-jacking that regularly took place on tour, when the famous trio would take over from any band that had been booked for our crew parties, with Hammond on base, May on keyboards and Clarkson on drums. You may have seen them when they performed in a special *Children in Need* episode of *Top Gear*. When they all manage to get in time with each other they are really quite good. When you were drunk, they always sounded fab.

Somehow we got back to the hotel and continued drinking with Hammond and May and Mindy and Sarah, James's and Richard's better halves. It was definitely morning when we eventually made it to bed and I have very rarely seen Jeremy in such a mess. I don't know how he managed it, but, like the

Duracell bunny that he is, he was off again, driving back to London to get himself ready for another crazy week ahead.

Chris Evans reared his ugly drinking head again when Jeremy and I were invited to his neighbour Adrian Newey's house for dinner. Adrian is hugely admired by Jeremy. He is one of the most successful designers in Formula 1 and motorsport in general, having won ten Constructors' World Championships, and seven different drivers have won the Formula 1 Drivers' World Championship with his designs.

We had a really fun evening on a perfect summer's night with another local celebrity, TV chef James Martin, also a petrolhead and a lovely guy. Despite being incredibly dyslexic and having had a tough start in life, with the education system failing him, James has not let that hold him back and has followed his passion, fighting through presenting fears to become really successful. Education was a big topic that night as, coincidentally, Jeremy had attended the same school as Adrian: Repton, a public school which they were both expelled from. Adrian went on to get a first-class honours degree in aeronautics and astronautics, and Jeremy … well, you know the rest. He continues to get rewarded for bad behaviour!

It was all quite civilised until Adrian, encouraged by Chris, decided to wheel out his trolley of vodka shots from around the world, a gift from his colleagues in F1. So, as if he were managing a pit stop, he wheeled the bespoke trolley to the edge of the table where Chris, who I was sitting next to, yet again coaxed me into downing several different shots. To be honest, I didn't need too much encouragement. I get terribly competitive and over-excited in these jolly party moments.

Yet, again, it ended badly. I love Chris Evans, I really do, and I miss socialising with him and Tash, but I do not miss the Pied Piper effect Chris has on me with alcohol. I was in real trouble with Jeremy, who accused me of flirting with Chris, which was not true at all. I was chatting to Tash just as much as to Chris, but the green-eyed monster in the big man was out and I was in the doghouse.

* * * *

Another time, that green-eyed monster popped out was at Mark and Katie Cecil's country retreat in Warwickshire. We had been invited to a summer lunch and a sleepover. Belle Robinson and Hamish Bullough were going, too; it was to be a bit of a Mustique reunion. By the way, if you can't remember who's who, you can Google most of the people I'm writing about.

As you have probably gathered by now, our life was very fast-paced and I often didn't know what I was going to and who was going to be there. This was one of those occasions. I met Jeremy up there and, as we walked into the Georgian manor at Priors Marston, he said, 'Andrew Ridgeley is going to be here, I think.'

'You think!' I thought, 'OMG!' My severe teenage crush was potentially staying in the same house we were in for the weekend and Jeremy just casually throws in that 'he might be there'. I would have liked to have been more prepared for that! I calmed myself as we were led out onto the terrace, looking over the croquet lawn and the lake beyond. The house was covered in lilac wisteria in full bloom. It could have been the most incredible romantic moment as I turned the corner and was introduced to the one who I thought was by far the better half of Wham!

However, seeing as I was with my boyfriend and Andrew had lost most of his hair (and what was left was grey), it was actually one of the weirdest moments of my life. There was my dream boy, now a skinny old man in a tweed jacket rather than a Fila tracksuit … what had happened?! Never meet your heroes, they say, or your heartthrobs, I say, especially when they look nothing like the poster you had on your bedroom ceiling years ago.

Now, most people in this grown-up and sophisticated situation would keep the fact that they were obsessed with the person they had just met to themselves, and I did. Jeremy, however, in his trouble-making way decided, out of nowhere, to tell Andrew about my teenage bedroom that was lined with Wham! posters, including a head shot of Andrew right over my bed. I wanted to disappear into the wisteria, but Andrew took it well – in fact, too well, and began to get rather amorous with me, enjoying the flattery in old age, I guess. He had been drinking for an hour or so more than us and it was only going to get worse.

Mark, our host, decided that we must visit the local pub for a pint, as you do, whilst his good wife finished all the preparations for lunch. Despite the alcohol taken, Jeremy volunteered to drive in the beast of a car he had for the weekend – I can't remember what it was. I was seriously distracted as I had Andrew Ridgeley practically sitting on my lap as we all crammed into the car and headed the short distance down the lane to the pub.

I had longed for this for years back in the eighties and I'd convinced myself back then that if Andrew had met me, he would want to marry me. I got so close when I was at one of the first Wham! concerts at the London Lyceum. We were right up front, leaning on the stage (this was the very early days of their career and concert security wasn't as it is now). I could touch Andrew's and George's legs that were exposed below their skimpy red-and-yellow shorts.

Now, in rural Warwickshire, it was too late; the moment had passed. Andrew had other ideas, though, and clung to me like I was the love of his life. Despite Jeremy having triggered this situation, he was now not happy about all the interest I was getting from Mr Ridgeley, but he didn't have to worry for long.

After one swift drink, Mark rounded us up and we headed back for lunch. I don't think Andrew even made it through his starter. He was later found asleep on the sofa in the drawing room and didn't surface till breakfast.

I have to finish this little episode by saying Andrew was actually lovely. His leanness was due to the fact that he's so fit – he's a fanatical cyclist. His drunkenness was probably due to the fact that he doesn't drink like that very often. Unlike someone else I know. All's well that ends well and I do actually have a treasured picture of us in a rather comical embrace.

But I won't be sticking it on my bedroom ceiling.

16

Next Stop, Venice

The next must-attend party-of-the-century was Sir Charles Dunstone's fiftieth. Was it to be in his swanky Holland Park London house, his Norfolk farmhouse, on board his beloved yacht, or would it be a private Caribbean island takeover? Well, Norfolk was voted out, but the yacht *Shemara* was to play a big part alongside what was *almost* an island takeover in the incredible city of Venice.

We were two of the lucky few hundred invited to Charles's fiftieth-birthday celebration weekend. We received an invitation in a gold envelope (gold-coloured, not actual gold – there were some limits to the budget). Enclosed were stylishly designed itinerary and information booklets and personalised leather luggage tags embossed with the *Shemara* logo.

We simply had to inform the event team organising the weekend what time we would be arriving at Marco Polo airport. We were greeted there by uniformed event management, who set us off in the right direction to board our pre-booked water taxi, a stylish Venetian speedboat, to take us to the world-famous Cipriani Hotel, where George Clooney and Amal Alamuddin had got married just a few months before.

The unique hotel, with the largest pool in Venice, dominates a small island in a prime location, pretty much opposite St Mark's Square, and offers views all around, across to other islands and iconic landmarks. It is set in beautiful rose-filled gardens and has a tennis court and several piers from which to set off for further exploration.

Our launch took us to a typical, picturesque Venetian jetty with its familiar candy-striped posts standing up out of the water, where we were met by more event personnel and the charming staff of the hotel. We were shown to our suite, courtesy of Sir Charles, who had taken over the entire hotel for his cast of party guests.

I say cast, as, yet again, there were celebs, lords and ladies popping up here, there and everywhere, probably not that different from the hotel's exciting beginnings in the late fifties. First stop, drinks on the terrace to meet fellow guests and get the party started. Jeremy was keen to just sit and soak up rosé all afternoon, but after some encouragement from fellow guests I persuaded him to take a boat to explore at least a little of Venice and to visit St Mark's Square. I had never been to Venice before, whereas Jeremy had got engaged to his first wife, Alex Hall, there. I wasn't sure whether it was awkward memories of his ex or his love of rosé that was causing his reluctance to venture forth from the hotel.

After a whistle-stop tour of St Mark's Square, we enjoyed a drink in unmissable Harry's Bar, where famous writers, artists, actors and aristocrats have hung out throughout its eighty-odd-year history – Hollywood icons Katharine Hepburn and Gary Cooper, writers Ernest Hemingway and Orson Welles, and so many more. It is a very unassuming celebrity haunt, incredibly basic and tiny, but known for its service, freedom and lack of imposition – perfect for Jezza to hide away and enjoy his favourite sport – drinking.

But it was time to head back to prepare for the warm-up party in the hotel. The Dunstones had thought of everything and there was even a marquee providing hair and make-up services for the ladies to perfect their party look. I declined as I'm not a fan of someone faffing around with my hair, even less my make-up; I prefer the *au naturel* look, and Friday night was supposed to be a little more low-key than the big ball planned for the following evening.

Or was it? We were guided down a small alleyway at the side of the hotel to the quay, where the great ship *Shemara* had been moored. The ancient cobbled quay was dressed with cocktail tables, candles and lights. Charles and Celia, dressed in nautically styled outfits, officially named their beloved yacht and speeches were given, while an endless supply of food and drink was circulated to all. We were then guided to a huge vaulted building, a former dockside warehouse, I assume, which had been transformed into a party venue. The entertainment for the evening was not some local Venetian musicians, but Duran Duran!

I had actually earlier spotted Gary Barlow sitting quietly on the terrace with his wife, Dawn, and had wondered if there was to be a full Take That reunion, but it was obvious now that he was just a guest. A guest that I ended up throwing some shapes with on the dance-floor along with his lovely wife, who, in my simple world of six degrees of separation, was part of the same dance troupe that my sister-in-law danced in. Gary and his wife Dawn are both incredibly unassuming and down to earth and great fun to dance with in front of Duran Duran – didn't see that coming!

Imagine turning up to your mate's fiftieth in your local village hall and you're dancing with Gary Barlow right in front of Simon Le Bon, just inches away from you – that's how intimate the evening was, but it wasn't a village hall, it was a great hall on the side of one of the most expensive hotels in Venice, dressed with chandeliers and lit for a full rock concert. Wow! What a start to an incredible weekend. The closing line on Friday night's itinerary was: 'The party tonight winds down at 2 a.m.' You can get a sense of the pace of the weekend!

We set our alarms that night to make sure we didn't miss the next event, which was a boat ride to another island and another takeover of a luxury venue, another of the Cipriani's delightful, unique settings, Locanda Cipriani. It was about an hour's boat ride away, but well worth the trip into a more rural setting through narrow canals surrounded by churches, pretty gardens and small, brightly coloured cottages.

In the light of day and before more rounds of alcohol, I was able to see who we were celebrating with: there were the usual suspects, such as Rebekah and Charlie Brooks, Liz Murdoch, Tony and Rita Gallagher and others from the Chipping Norton Set; Simon and Yasmin Le Bon; a whole bunch of retail giants, including Sir Stuart Rose, former chairman of Marks & Spencer and Ocado; luxury handbag designer Anya Hindmarch and her husband and business partner, James; and Sir Philip and Lady Green. Sir Philip had a pop at Jeremy for his dress sense, which prompted me to point out to him that he had a crease ironed into his jeans. I asked, 'When was *that* ever in fashion? Surely, you should know better!' He did not like that, but I'm not afraid to speak up, sir or no sir. It was very disappointing that he didn't have a sense of humour, that while he was quite happy dishing out insults, he wasn't happy to take them. Probably not a surprise to most of you, given his history.

A favourite guest of mine was the founder of Ted Baker, Ray Kelvin CBE, and his wife Clare. Ray was desperate to get Jeremy into one of his old-fashioned barbers, Ted's Grooming Room, back in London. No chance.

There was a woman from *The Only Way is Essex*, or some equally terrible TV programme, but I can't remember her name, which, of course, she would be devastated about. It seemed her main aim in life was to get attention. (Ooh, you're getting the dark side of me, but I'm not keen on people obsessed with their image – you probably guessed that as I'd chosen Jeremy as my beau.)

*   *   *   *

Back to Locanda. It was the perfect lunch, seated in the shade of grapevines and flowering climbers, followed by a rather comical boat ride back to the Cipriani. Boarding small boats whilst drunk is not advisable, nor is travelling at speed across choppy water after eating a lot of food.

There was just enough time for an afternoon snooze before preparing for the big night. The Chipping Norton Set had agreed to meet in the hotel bar by the pool for pre-voyage drinks. We were to meet at the hotel's jetty at specific times to take water taxis to a surprise venue.

There was great excitement in the air; more guests were arriving, including the hilarious Johnny Vaughan, former *Big Breakfast* presenter and Capital radio DJ. He went into one of his genius patters, suggesting Jeremy was a lesbian. 'All the signs are there,' he said. I think the whole ramble was triggered by Jeremy having grown a beard, and Johnny suggested he was having hormone treatment. 'I knew it,' he said, 'it's obvious, look at him.' He went on at his usual incredible fast pace. 'Look at him,' he said. 'Sensible shoes, manly job, ill-fitting jeans, tinkering with cars, but always hanging around women! He's definitely a lesbian!' he declared. Jeremy and I were crying with laughter. Johnny is my number-one guest for a fantasy dinner party, him and his non-stop entertainment. A nightmare to live with, I imagine, but the best guest.

It was time to go. We ended up sharing a water taxi with Simon and Yasmin Le Bon and Johnny, who continued to entertain us. He is one of Charles's oldest friends; they were at school together, along with David Ross, at Uppingham, a public school. Johnny was lined up to do an after-dinner speech. I couldn't wait for that. Amid the endless banter from Johnny, I ended up having Simon Le Bon fastening the back of my dress. I did not see that coming, nor had I imagined just how incredible the evening was going to be.

We arrived at a disused jetty and what looked like a run-down warehouse, but this was no ordinary disused jetty and warehouse. It wasn't a Carphone one either. (Sorry, couldn't resist that: in case you don't know, Charles co-founded Carphone Warehouse.) The Dunstones' event team, armed with an enormous budget, had dressed the almost derelict site to create what felt like another mind-blowing film set, which included a red carpet that led from the water-taxi drop-off into a fantasy reception area dressed with huge drapes and including a faux tapestry depicting Charles's life, like something you'd see in a castle, showing the story of the many ancestors who had gone before.

It had a kind of *Where's Wally* feel to it; it was great fun to spot things like Five Guys burger joints (that was Charles's latest business venture) alongside his America's Cup yacht, TalkTalk offices and Carphone Warehouse outlets and, of course, Charles's pride and joy, the great yacht *Shemara*. It also reminded me of the angst Jeremy and I had had over what to buy the man who, literally, has everything. Present ideas are something that I am good at, though; I was even complimented by Jeremy on my skill, and asked to think of and find presents for his daughters. I came up with the perfect gift for Sir Charles: cufflinks.

I can hear you groaning. But these were no ordinary cufflinks; the friends that I mentioned earlier, who I used to live with, were high-end jewellers and I had asked them if they could make cufflinks in the shape of *Shemara*. At a cost, yes, was the answer. I managed to persuade Jeremy, who, as I've said before, is not good at parting with money, that if he thought about the value of all the dinners, parties, holidays and long weekends we'd had courtesy of the Dunstones that the large price to pay for these very special cufflinks, with diamonds creating the portholes on *Shemara*, was a very small price considering all we had had from Charles. For me, the best reward for making the effort to organise such a special gift was the look on Charles's face when he received them.

Back to the birthday bash of the century. After a champagne reception, we were led through to a dining hall with a specially designed table forming a giant S shape to create a more intimate feel for the hundreds of guests. The entire venue was candle-lit and decorated with hundreds of red roses as centrepieces and huge podium displays. Even the waiting staff were beautiful and performed a perfectly choreographed entrance to deliver the food. It was all party perfection.

After dinner, there was another reveal as curtains opened and Gary Barlow appeared, along with a grand piano. Disappointingly for me, not with the rest of Take That, but, let's face it, Gary's the one with the most talent. So, yet again, I was up close and personal with yet another king of pop, crooning along with him as well as all the other women at the party.

As Gary finished off with a song performed to Charles's mother, who joined him on stage, it was time for another big reveal as more drapes were removed to invite us through to a pop-up nightclub, where I totally disgraced myself by dancing with and manhandling Piers Morgan. I wanted to dislike him because Jeremy hated him so much, but he seemed a genuinely charming guy and was very tolerant of a very drunk me.

I have no idea what time it was that we got to bed, except that it was light and Jeremy insisted on going back to the hotel bar for just one more drink with the boys. At some point during the morning, Jeremy finally made it to bed, not to surface till the afternoon, when we realised we'd missed the poolside brunch and were actually slightly panicked that we may have missed our flight home. We scrambled ourselves together and made it poolside just in time to scrape up a few leftovers of yet more incredible food, but this time without alcohol – not for me anyway, but the big man is hardcore and was straight in for a hair of the dog.

Now that's what I call a party!

* * * *

Back home and back to reality, I took my dad and my boy for a mini-break in Devon and slowed down for a while until the *Top Gear Tour* was off to Norway again. Weekends in the winter were often filled with the age-old country pursuit of pheasant shooting. My first ever pheasant shoot was in my home county, Hertfordshire, at a country estate about ten miles from my house, which belonged to a relative of the lovely Nick Allott. I was invited to join the shooting party for lunch and, after much consideration, because I really don't like killing anything, I decided to go out with Jeremy on the afternoon drives. That doesn't mean driving cars, it means driving the pheasants out of the woods and up into the air to meet their fate.

Jeremy taught me to load his gun, so I wasn't just standing idle, also with the aim of him being able to shoot more. Having got my head round it, I felt that it was okay for the birds to die because they'd had a nice life, roaming freely and were fed daily by a sinister gamekeeper (gamekeepers are always sinister) to then be eaten and appreciated. What I couldn't cope with was if they were not killed outright and were flailing around suffering.

I became obsessed with watching each struck bird to make sure it was dead and was therefore a terribly bad loader. Luckily, Jeremy saw the funny side of this, unlike Rowan Atkinson's wife's reaction over an earlier incident. Yes, Rowan Atkinson was there too. It would be poor form to have just one celeb on your shoot.

Poor Rowan had unwittingly let his dogs out of the car whilst getting something to prepare for the afternoon. One of them had run off and killed one of the host's prize hens. Most of the shooting party thought this quite amusing, but Sunetra, Rowan's wife, was so cross with him and embarrassed, as I would have been had it been my husband.

Rowan, who is naturally quite a quiet man, went into his shell even more, Mr Bean-like, as he sat with his head down in the back of the Land Rover that was ferrying us all to the next shoot site. I felt quite sorry for him and ended up walking with him as his angry wife strode ahead with Jeremy. Another bizarre moment that I could never have imagined, comforting one of the best-known comedy actors in the world whilst trudging through a muddy field.

* * * *

Soon Christmas was upon us. Jeremy and I spent it with our respective families, but we had an amazing New Year trip to look forward to.

The Dunstones had invited us to join them in the Caribbean for a week's cruise on the beautiful *Shemara*. We were to join fellow shipmates Rebekah and Charlie Brooks, an old friend of Sir Charles, Nick and his wife Lucy from Norfolk, the county where the Dunstones have a country house, and another couple whose names I'm ashamed to say I cannot for the life of me remember. (I blame it on age and alcohol!)

Of course, I'd had a preview of this beautiful floating palace whilst we partied on her in St Tropez, but it had been crammed with party people and I had been crammed with alcohol, so I hadn't really taken it all in and hadn't seen the full glory of it. We'd seen her in Venice, too, but we had missed the opportunity to have the guided tour that was on offer while she was docked. We were probably asleep or drunk on that occasion.

Now it was time to be fully immersed in luxury life on one of the most beautiful yachts in the world. It was hard not to keep gasping in awe at the luxury and elegance of every inch of this dream cruiser, now sailing in the idyllic climate and scenery of the Caribbean.

I'd never had a desire to go cruising. I didn't fancy being cooped up in a floating hotel and I'd imagined it would get boring, looking at the sea endlessly, let alone worrying about seasickness. With Charles and Celia in charge there was no fear of any of that.

They had not compromised on anything. The elegant charm of the original thirties *Shemara* had been carefully preserved and restored to an incredible standard, blended with modern comfort, design and technology. It had a stabilising system to help prevent any discomfort and seasickness in rough seas, its own desalinating system to provide an endless supply of water, and modern Rolls-Royce diesel-electric engines.

Anyway, enough about all the specs. As you might imagine, our social life was not at all boring. We soon settled into life aboard, enjoying pre-dinner cocktails in the upper bar, moving down to the elegant dining room below or, if the evenings were warm enough, out on deck around another huge dining table. Everything was perfect, even down to the sugar lumps for our tea, which were moulded into miniature teapots.

During the week, as usual in this crowd, there was loads going on. We went snorkelling – there was diving equipment, but we didn't venture that deep – we relaunched rescued turtles and enjoyed most of the essential superyacht toys, such as a giant floating raft which was towed at speed behind the tender, and seabobs – hand-held jet devices that propel you through the water, James Bond-style. Charles, Charlie and Nick took the small sailboat out for a spin and tested out the paddleboards and kayaks. The toy of all toys was the inflatable waterslide that rolled out over the side of the boat. That was great fun, hurtling twenty-odd feet down into the warm Caribbean sea. We cruised into deserted bays, where, magically, a solitary beach bar was open for us – its only customers. As I've said before, I so often felt like I was on a film set whilst on these extraordinary adventures.

The only upset out at sea was finding the bay Charles had selected to anchor in for the night had another stunning thirties yacht moored, but with two funnels, which seemingly trumped *Shemara*. It turned out it was Tara Getty (brother-in-law to Domi, with whom Jeremy and I had stayed in Italy and descendant of the infamous J Paul Getty, founder of Getty Oil). After Charles got over not having the bay to himself and perhaps feeling a bit sore that Tara's boat was bigger than his, it was soon decided that if you can't beat them, join them! It was arranged that we would visit *Talitha*, Tara's yacht, named after his mother, for early-evening drinks with all the Getty family aboard and their guests.

You couldn't make it up. How did I land in this world? But yet again I had a personal connection with one of my newfound friends in this extraordinary world. A guest on the Gettys' yacht worked with my sister-in-law on QVC, possibly the weirdest six degrees of separation in this story so far. A luxury-silk-flower seller on board the yacht of one of the world's most famous wealthy families in a tiny bay in the Caribbean!

We all had a guided tour of *Talitha*, which was, in fact, bigger than *Shemara*, but by just under twenty metres. A lot of boat-off banter ensued as, although *Shemara* was smaller, she was way ahead in terms of technical spec, and *Talitha* was looking really tired. It was a bit like being on the actual *Titanic*, as it didn't appear to have been renovated since the thirties. It was a bit like visiting your grandma's house that's stuck in a time warp. (That is, if your grandma is the Queen.) And here's some extra Getty trivia: Tara's full name is Tara Gabriel Galaxy Gramophone Getty. I think his parents may have been under the influence of something special when they registered the poor boy's name. I have to say that he and his family were delightfully down to earth and were fully aware of their privileged life and made the best of it.

* * * *

Next port of call was Mustique for New Year's Eve celebrations, where we would meet up with the Cecils, Belle and Hamish and several hundred other Mustique residents. The party of all parties on Mustique for New Year was at the Beach Club below the Cotton House (the club house of the island, where residents regularly meet and island issues are dealt with).

There was that usual New Year air of excitement aboard *Shemara* amongst us and we all dressed up accordingly, only then to be blown and bounced about on the tender that we had to take to get us to the island. The downside to luxury yachting is that you don't get to turn up shoreside looking immaculate, but you do look cool arriving on a private island just for the evening, having weaved in and out of several luxury vessels all anchored for the evening's celebrations.

As with so many New Year parties, it was a bit of a disappointment. Everyone got split up in the drunken crowds as the entire population of Mustique descended on the purpose-built tented village around the beach bar, which included an outdoor cinema for the children's entertainment. Jeremy was off his face and had scuttled off with some of his best party buddies, so I felt totally deflated as the fireworks decorated the Caribbean sky and the new year began.

Tending to our hangovers over a very late breakfast, all of us ship-mates decided that we preferred our own social life in the divine comfort of *Shemara*.

We had a lot of laughs with our new friends, Lucy and Nick, who was like Jeremy's long-lost twin, matching him at six-foot five-inches and incredibly funny, with a passion for drinking too. He was a real character, who loved his food. One of his funniest stories was describing how he had used to travel up and down the UK as a salesman with a full set of condiments – tomato sauce, mustard, relishes, salt and pepper etc. – in the side-door pocket of his car. Jeremy thought he was one of the funniest men he'd ever met, and even suggested they might write together.

One of our *Shemara* parties ended with the two giants and little ol' Charlie Brooks dad-dancing around the jacuzzi at the bow of the boat. When those kids weren't entertaining us, the Dunstones' children and Rebekah and Charlie's little girl were a great source of fun too.

On the night of New Year's Day, we enjoyed another delicious dinner in the elegance of the formal dinning room, complete with its portrait of the Queen. We snuggled down in the living room, watching a film under the lights of the Christmas tree. Yes, a full-height proper tree and a TV screen that was disguised as a mirror above the fireplace.

It was hard to leave the luxury and hospitality of *Shemara* and her crew and our fellow ship-mates, but not too hard, as Jeremy and I had tagged on a couple of nights in a boutique hotel in Antigua, a gentle descent back to normality, without a full complement of staff to tend to our every need.

17

2015, Year of the Punch

As you're reading, or listening to, this book, you are more than likely a fan, or at least very much aware, of Jeremy Clarkson, so will undoubtedly know that he punched a TV producer and was subsequently dismissed or, as Jeremy likes to point out, his contract was not renewed. What some of you will not be aware of was that some of the most senior people at the BBC were trying to save him and the very lucrative brand he had created (along with more than a little help from his friends), but he completely blew any hope of redemption one night at a high-profile charity dinner.

The wonderful Nick Allott had invited Jeremy and me (well, mainly Jeremy, of course) to the Roundhouse Gala Dinner. This was one of those events that needed high-profile guests to gain press interest and help with the fundraising. The evening's proceeds were to go to the Roundhouse Trust, which gives thousands of eleven- to twenty-five-year-olds the chance to develop their performing-art skills, and which supports them as they do so.

It was another wall-to-wall celeb event. We were on a table with Nick and Christa, our Mykonos hosts, Sir Tim Rice, whom

I had the pleasure of sitting next to and, yet again, the old six degrees popped up, as Sir Tim had grown up very close to my childhood home, so we both used to swim in the same pool in a tiny village close to where I live now. Strange, but true. There was also Christopher Biggins and his partner Neil, and Nick and Nettie Mason.

There was top entertainment from Jamie Cullum, the Stereophonics and Sharleen Spiteri from the band Texas, who jammed with Ronnie Wood. It was quite a night.

Christopher Biggins hosted the auction, which had incredible items such as a seven-night stay on Richard Branson's Necker Island; some Rolling Stones collector's items, including Ronnie Woods's guitar and Charlie Watts's drumsticks; lunch with the Monty Python cast; and a meet-and-greet with Chelsea FC's first team at their training ground.

It was decided over dinner, as a last-minute addition, that Jeremy would offer up the last ever lap around the *Top Gear* track, with the help of his friend Nick Mason from Pink Floyd, who offered his million-pound LaFerrari for the ultimate lap experience.

At this point in the 'punch saga', Jeremy had been suspended, but a decision hadn't been reached about his future. It was rumoured that Tony Hall, the director-general of the BBC at the time, was very keen to keep the big man. Jeremy undoubtedly brought in good money for the corporation.

However, once Jeremy got up on stage with Nick Mason to pitch his offer of a day at the track, he was heavily infused with alcohol and went on to deliver a rant heavy on expletives, describing his frustration with the BBC and his bosses and how they had ruined his show. He ranted on, assuming and referring to, his imminent sacking.

Jeremy bounced back to the table through the throng of rousing support and announced that I'd be great at organising all concerned for the big day. Cheers, Jezza! Another unpaid treat for me. To be honest, it was an honour and I dutifully put everything in place to ensure the generous donors had a great day out. The guys who generously bid for the track day of a lifetime planned to take their sons along too. Can you imagine how highly they would have regarded their dads from then on?

To add to the never-ending fallout from that infamous punch, unbeknown to Jeremy on that fateful evening, a *Mirror* journalist was at the event and the whole rant was reported, with a video recording. And that is what I and others in the centre of the storm believed sealed his fate. Jeremy had just pushed the boundaries too far and run out of BBC lives.

Outside there were paparazzi, who were following us constantly at this time, and a huge throng of them, along with TV stations and satellite vans, were camped outside Jeremy's flat in Holland Park for a week. It was a very stressful, intense time. On this particular evening when a photographer was literally lying across the bonnet of my car with his flash going off constantly so I couldn't see. Jeremy was shouting at me, 'Just drive!' It was not pleasant. I'd love to know what the legal position is if you drive away while someone is deliberately trying to prevent you doing so, by lying on your bonnet. Would it have been legal to have run him over? Or at least pushed him gently to the kerb with my front grille!?

The last lap at the track went really well. A massive £100,000 was raised for the Roundhouse charity and Jeremy got the choice of Nick Mason's million-pound beast, a Ferrari 488 GTB and a Mercedes AMG GTS to spin around the track for the last, rather emotional time. Unfortunately, Jeremy and I had had a huge row and, despite it promising to be a really important and nostalgic day for me too, I had to stand my ground and didn't go.

In order to escape constant hounding by the press, somewhat ironically but very kindly, Rebekah Brooks offered us her house in the privacy of the Brooks family estate in the Chipping Norton Golden Triangle. We spent the weekend there, and for the first time ever during this incredibly stressful period, Jeremy relaxed, collapsed and slept most of the time, finally exhausted by his never-ending controversial battles with the Beeb.

Strangely, it was something he and Andy Wilman said they would miss, battling with the PC army within the very institution that they were so proud to be working for. It was a definite love-hate relationship, but finally Jeremy and Andy's united front of old school friends bending the rules had been forced to retreat.

*   *   *   *

Now Jeremy was unemployed, there was definitely time to fit in another holiday to Mustique. Belle and Hamish had yet again extended their generosity and invited us out to Hibiscus, their beautiful colonial-style property. Jeremy really needed a retreat and our hosts were very happy for him to just rest in the privacy of the villa. The first night, the big man was showing his vulnerability and, crestfallen, he actually decided to stay in and have a quiet evening, catching up with our favourite box set, *Game of Thrones*.

However, unsurprisingly, Jezza was soon revved up, albeit with huge bravado, and we were out on the party scene once more. We'd had one particularly big night already. Our intention this evening was the opposite. We went out early to Basil's Bar on the water to watch the sunset with Belle and Hamish, had dinner at the Cecils – there were just eight of us – after which Jeremy and I decided to call it a night. The big man was definitely feeling the strain of the last month or so. Rather downbeat, we headed back to Hibiscus, whilst Hamish and Belle went on to seek further entertainment at another party.

Jeremy and I pulled up in our allocated space in our Flintstone-mobile back at Hibiscus, looked at each other and Jeremy said, 'Shall we go back out and find them?'

The party beast just couldn't be kept down. After whizzing around the island for a while looking for our comrades we very nearly crashed into David Ross taking a drunken, wide turn into the driveway to his hidden luxury lair. We were literally face to face in our open-sided vehicles and wheel to wheel, but I made use of the unwanted meeting and asked, 'Have you seen Belle and Hamish?' He informed us they had gone rogue and were on the 'wrong side' of the island at the only 'underground' nightclub on Mustique, largely frequented by the locals and all the staff employed by each household. Set amongst the island workforce's residential houses was an empty bungalow where the main living space had been turned into a dance-floor. Well, who'd have imagined Jezza enjoying a bit of bump and grind till the early hours, and there wasn't even any organic rosé to fuel him.

Yet again the night ran into the morning before we made it to bed; we had managed to socialise and drink literally from sunset to sunrise. That morning the 9 a.m. breakfast rule was broken even by Belle herself. And one of the funniest breakfast moments ever occurred when Hamish, having finally stumbled out and slumped down, holding his head with one hand and pouring orange juice with the other, spectacularly and completely missed his glass as if it wasn't there at all and poured orange juice all over the table. He just kept pouring. His reactions weren't just slow, they weren't there at all!

I'd arranged for the lovely Shaun Woodward to come for coffee at Hibiscus and deliver some sage advice to the disgraced, broken and confused star. Jeremy and I had discussed at length his options. Believe it or not, deep down, Jeremy is a man of simple pleasures and he always repeated a little life mantra when thinking about not earning so much money in return for an easier life: he said, 'You only need one watch.' He was also set on selling his beloved Mercedes C63 AMG Black and buying a simple Golf GTI. We even discussed living away from the Chipping Norton area and having just a regular-sized country house.

Shaun agreed with me that Jeremy should take a well-earned break and think about what he really wanted. For a nanosecond in the workaholic's high-speed life, he seriously considered life in the slow lane and a less-is-more approach to life. But as we all know, he got straight back in the fast lane, as only an adrenaline junkie would.

Traditional Mustique life took hold and we indulged in back-to-back lunches, dinners and parties. All the usual party people were right behind the big man, with many suggesting that anyone could be forgiven for losing it enough to hit someone who had annoyed you when you were under extreme pressure. I wasn't so sure and became increasingly worried about him unravelling further. I wasn't alone in having concerns. Adrian and Nicola Gill felt the same and supported me in trying to encourage the high-speed juggernaut to at least move over to the middle lane.

Back home, it seemed that Jeremy worked harder than ever, but in a very different vein. He often quipped he had become a businessman and a hard negotiator, claiming he learnt everything from Richard Gere in the film *Arbitrage*. Clarkson, Hammond, May and Wilman, by their own admission, had to grow up.

The fab four's new-found business acumen served them well and we all know the rest of the story. They actually had a lot of fun setting up their own production company called W. Chump & Sons Ltd (W for Wilman, C for Clarkson, H for Hammond, U for *und* (the German word for 'and', used just to make it work), M for May and P for production). They also invested in company cars, three Reliant Robins branded with their new company name. All those cars did was cause traffic jams in London, as they kept breaking down.

Party invitations kept rolling in and there were regular star-studded dinners at Belle Robinson's, plenty of birthday bashes too. It never ceased to amaze me how many rich and/or famous and powerful people Jeremy knew. We partied at the home of Christiane Amanpour, the highly regarded international anchor for CNN. Christiane is married to James Rubin, a former American diplomat and assistant secretary of state for public affairs in the Clinton administration. God help us, he's a party animal!

* * * *

Speaking of which, I met Boris Johnson on a couple of occasions, most memorably at one of the most bizarre Christmas parties I'd ever been to, of the sort which were a regular highlight during the festive season for many of the great and good, also the frankly bad.

Evgeny Lebedev, the son of Russian oligarch and former KGB agent Alexander Lebedev, put on more celebtastic events than even Jimmy Carr. Evgeny owns the *Evening Standard*, *The Independent* and the TV channel London Live. It was rumoured that he would invite any big name in order to build his media empire. Well, you would, wouldn't you?

These were truly extraordinary events. The Christmas parties were held in his apartment near Regent's Park and were renowned for the giant bowl of caviar put out as the main party nibble. You literally had to fight your way to it. One year it became the butt of jokes, since it had obviously been affected by the recent austerity measures as the bowl was considerably smaller than the year before.

At one of these bizarre events, I met Sir Tony Hall, who was talking to Dame Shirley Bassey, who was accompanied by a young man, the concierge from her hotel. She had basically hired him as her companion for the evening. He was remarkably cool and calm given the mind-blowing circumstances. Imagine when he got home from his shift at the hotel, his partner asking, 'What did you do today?' It was a bit different from getting some theatre tickets or booking a VIP car for a guest. Literally at every turn, you would bump into a very familiar face, and it wasn't a big place. I was literally rubbing body parts, not just shoulders, with the likes of Graham Norton, George Osborne, David Cameron and Samantha, James Blunt, Stephen Fry and, relatively new to this extraordinary social circle, Idris Elba, who had brought his PA along with him for company. She suddenly interrupted the conversation between Jeremy, Idris and me. She was in a slight state of shock, announcing, 'See that woman over there in the black fur? Guess what it's made out of?' She couldn't contain herself for more than a second, still suffering from the shock of her discovery. 'Gorilla,' she said, and her mouth and eyes remained open wide.

It makes me feel sick now. After that shocking information, Jeremy and I decided to leave, despite the fact that I'd earlier been having a very different, lovely chat with James Blunt, about prams. His wife had not long before given birth to their first baby. Mr Blunt is a properly nice chap.

Jeremy was not a great fan of these parties, but felt he should show his face and I think he felt peer pressure from his immediate circle of friends. You may wonder how he came to be invited to all these parties. A lot of the invitations came about in the clichéd way of 'I'll talk to his people'. If you're in the fame game, invitations are constantly fired out to PAs and managers alike, especially for promoting new products and generally for constant networking.

Evgeny must have rated Jeremy as one of his 'special ones' because we got invited to his villa in Italy for a long weekend, though unfortunately it clashed with something else. We did make dinner at his Hampton Court home, though, which was another incredible evening.

As was so often the case, Adrian and Nicola were amongst the guests. It was always a comfort to me to have some true friends for moral support at what could sometimes be rather overwhelming events.

After drinks out on the picturesque rose-scented terrace of what was once one of Henry VIII's hunting lodges, we moved in to be seated for dinner, or should I say a banquet. I always got a little nervous as to who I was going to be sitting next to, but on this occasion Jeremy and I were sitting next to one another and opposite Michael Gambon, whom I'd met before, not that he'd remember – his ageing memory was letting him down. However, Philippa, his 'other woman' always remembered me, as another 'other woman'.

To the left of Philippa was Harry Enfield, who, once we'd settled in to the banquet asked me, 'And how do you fit into this?' as he gesticulated towards Jeremy. He knew Jeremy's wife and was obviously wondering who I was. Quite boldly, and tongue-in-cheek, I answered, 'I'm the other woman,' to which he swiftly added, 'Then, I shall call you Whore,' in one of his finest voices. Everyone fell about laughing, including myself. Thinking about the venue we were in, it was actually quite fitting, and I can imagine those very words being uttered at a Tudor banquet, at which no doubt many shenanigans went on.

18

Turkish Delights

The next time I saw dear Harry [Enfield] was at the launch of Soho House, Istanbul. A bit like Charles Dunstone's fiftieth, this was a double-header. All the usual suspects were there: Adrian and Nicola; Jemima Khan; Charles and Celia Dunstone; Nick Allott and Christa; fellow restaurateur and hotelier Jeremy King and his interior designer wife Lauren; and Alice B-B and Nick Love, who I haven't written much about, but they are two of the loveliest people I met during this roller-coaster period of of my life. We keep in touch.

Alice is editor-at-large for *Country and Town House* and *The Times*'s *Luxx* magazine and is well worth following on Instagram to see all her amazing travel adventures. Nick is a talented film director responsible for epics like *The Sweeney* and *The Firm*. He once filmed with the *Top Gear* trio, creating a Sweeney-style car chase, which ended with Hammond blowing the wrong caravan up and writing off a Jaguar XFR.

Jeremy was very fond of Alice, describing her as the most gentle, sweetest girl, which she is. He was also very fond of Nick and they had a lot of banter together. Nick is a real East End boy done good. He's a recovering alcoholic and drug addict who tried to encourage Jeremy to clean up his act too, but to no avail.

My attempts at trying to get Jeremy to slow down and give up his hardcore party habits were not going well. With one of his worst partners in crime, Richard Bacon, attending this mega-party weekend out in Istanbul, I stood no chance.

It was another star-studded event, with the first night being a gentle warm-up at the roof-terrace bar, which was so cool with its rooftop pool. It does get a little blurry as to what happened when, but the big night was dinner in the grand ballroom, with after-dinner entertainment by Paloma Faith, who was fantastic, dancing and singing on the tables, weaving her way through all the diners.

Ant and Dec were there with their respective partners. I was so pleased to meet them and was so shocked to discover how humble they were. They explained that they felt a little out of place at such a star-studded do. Who'd have thought? I actually felt a little the same, but in my case understandably so. It was a very showy event, with loads of air-kissing and smoke-blowing in the nether regions. I preferred to sit chatting with Ant and Dec and their partners, talking about our pet dogs. They explained that they had been invited because they had just invested in Soho House, Chiswick.

At some point, I was also very drunk with the nation's favourite duo and Clarkson made some joke out of me towering over them, as I was around six-foot three-inches in my party heels.

Hilarious Harry Enfield spotted me from afar and called out, 'Ah, Whore! How nice to see you!' I loved being insulted by one of my favourite comedians. What an honour!

I had a total starstruck moment when Jeremy and I got into a very small lift with Eddie Redmayne and his wife. I'd just watched him in *The Theory of Everything* and felt compelled to tell him how brilliant he was. He was very charming and gracious. Jeremy, however, was really cross with me for being groupie-like and apologised to Eddie on my behalf, which, in my opinion, was more embarrassing and out of order. As you might imagine, Jeremy and I often argued. I stood up for myself on numerous occasions and wasn't afraid to put the big man in his place.

Other big names were Jamie Dornan, Luke Evans, Professor Green, Millie Mackintosh, Daisy Lowe, Eliza Doolittle and Henry Holland – all a bit cool for school for me and Jeremy had no idea who they were. I certainly knew who Kit Harington was: my favourite *Game of Thrones* star. Sophie Ellis-Bextor, Pixie Geldof, Fearne Cotton, Claudia Winkleman and Radio 1 DJ Nick Grimshaw were all there to celebrate the grand opening. Mr Grimshaw was up all night and batting off complaints from other, more mature guests, who did not appreciate his party antics.

Jamie Theakston, another of my teen TV heroes, and his wife Sophie hung out with Jeremy and me for a large part of one evening. Sophie used to work for Soho House, starting in her late teens, and told me how she used to be sent out to get drugs for the guests. On hearing this, my jaw fell open, but I don't think she noticed as she wobbled about on her liquid supper. I am quite naive about drugs. I just don't understand why the police don't carry out more raids on places that are known as drug dens, but I'm guessing I won't be very popular for saying that since I've learnt indulging in drugs is as common as having a cup of tea in the world of TV and showbiz, and, these days, on any high street's social scene.

Anyhow, without the aid of drugs, unlike most of the guests, I had an amazing time, although got my alcohol quota spectacularly wrong on the first night and found myself struggling to leave the bathroom the next morning in order to get ready to go on the next adventure that our host Nick Jones, founder of Soho House and husband of newscaster Kirsty Young, had organised. It would have been frowned upon, especially by Jeremy, for me not to turn up. So, I scraped myself together and met everyone down at the quayside for a boat trip up the river Bosphorus for lunch.

Yes, a river cruise: the perfect cure for a seriously *baaad* hangover. Not!! I was genuinely worried that I might throw up at any time in front of many of my favourite screen heroes. I took myself to the back of the boat and tried to work out whether to sit or lie down. I soon gained the sympathy of Ant, Dec, Lisa and Ali. Lisa saved me. On observing my fragile state, she said, 'Would you like a beef Hula Hoop?'

'OMG, yes!' I said. 'That's exactly what I need to soak up the alcohol overflow and settle my stomach.'

Lisa said, 'I always pick them up in the airport.'

I had to laugh at that because this was what I had to do when on tour with *Top Gear*. Beef Hula Hoops were part of James May's rider.

I've always loved Ant and Dec, but they went way up in my estimation after I had been hanging out with them – literally, hanging. And all credit to Lisa, who is a genuinely nice person. I'm very sad they didn't succeed in running the marriage gauntlet, but all appears to have worked out for the best.

I survived the boat trip, concentrating very hard all the while on not being sick. Jeremy had no sympathy; he just laughed, and laughed harder when I couldn't face the delicious lunch we were all treated to at a riverside restaurant.

Luckily, I was sitting next to a kind and fascinating man, Jason McCue, the husband of Mariella Frostrup. Jason is a top lawyer specialising in human rights and civil liberties, no stranger to entering war zones and consulting with heads of states and governments. He would not look out of place in a

Bond movie with his rugged good looks, but throws a strong Warrington (northern) accent, which somehow doesn't fit with his character, intriguing me further. I wish I hadn't been so jaded; I would have loved to have learnt more about his incredible life.

*　　*　　*　　*

Jeremy loved all the eclectic characters he mixed with whilst travelling the world. For a man so well-travelled, I found it so endearing that he got excited by touching down in yet another airport and that he was still always keen to explore.

In some free time from our intense party schedule, we went off exploring the back streets of Istanbul and met Nicola and Adrian to peruse the famous Grand Bazaar. Most of you would not have recognised Clarkson, the bombastic, opinionated TV personality, as he marvelled at the hundreds of beautiful coloured lanterns and stroked and poked at the piles of artisan rugs and fabrics. He declared we would go back and fill a container to furnish and decorate our planned farmhouse back in the Cotswolds.

You may have got wind of his flair for interior design when he chatted cushions with Will Young on *Top Gear* and they joked about having a makeover programme together. And that's a hint of what I called the REAL Jeremy Clarkson, who sadly got lost in the whirlwind of work and celebrity social la-la land.

We finished up our Istanbul adventure with a final boozy lunch on the roof terrace of the incredible venue, a former US-embassy building, which had stunning original features. Nick Jones and his team have fully restored the incredible building to its original glamour, including hand-painted frescoes and Corinthian columns, brought up to date with

Soho House cool. Jeremy and I would highly recommend a stay in the heart of that multicultural city, to feel the vibe of the once major trading hub that was an integral part of the Silk Road. With or without wall-to-wall celebs, Istanbul will stimulate all your senses.

19

The Naughty Table

Back home, it was time to rebrand the notorious trio so that they could complete the live-show tour. It became known simply as *Clarkson, Hammond and May Live*. I looked after them all as we toured and they performed in their live arena shows in Sheffield, Belfast and South Africa, whilst they negotiated their future with Amazon.

Jeremy and I were also meeting builders and architects and planning our future home out at what you all now know as 'Clarkson's Farm'. Sheffield and Belfast had been a great source of research into Georgian style as we, along with the rest of the entourage, had stayed in exclusive manor houses. I bought Jeremy some Georgian architecture books to help us decide on details of doors, flooring, columns and balustrades. He enjoyed working on the design and it was a great and timely distraction from partying.

We had another luxury holiday in the South of France, but it was not terribly relaxing. Jeremy, after years of burning the candle hard and fast at both ends – and in the middle – was finally coming to terms with the need to change. Andy Wilman,

Jeremy's children and I persuaded him to slow down a little to help start his new future with Amazon.

This meant that, rather than peacefully relaxing on holiday, which of course involved drinking, he was on edge, thinking about life without any alcohol at all and all the other toxic habits that went with it. It was a bit of an emotional, drunk then sober, weird roller-coaster of a holiday.

Talking of sobriety, I once attended a party without Jeremy at Jemima's London home, for Nicola Formby's birthday, I think. It was a lovely evening and Nicola and I observed how many recovering alcoholics and drug addicts were there (obviously not drinking, or taking drugs). We realised what a lovely evening it had been: still a lot of fun, but with no drama and without guests disappearing to 'fuel their habits'.

On a funny note, I did have to laugh, as did Adrian Gill, when Jimmy Carr suggested that in this interim time before Jeremy relaunched himself with Amazon, he should go and get his teeth, hair and face sorted out. Can you imagine Jeremy Clarkson with gleaming white teeth, a full head of neatly coiffured hair, and with a chiselled jawline!!?? I think that would be more terrifying than the current dishevelled look of an upper-class tramp!

Even his fellow party comrades knew he was pushing the boundaries too far and supported me in encouraging him to make some changes. Many of them felt it was time for him to grow up and slow down a little. It was a challenging time, especially when the party invitations kept flying in.

Jeremy did begin to prioritise which parties he really should attend and a couple spring to mind that stood out. One was a birthday bash for Jemima Khan, put on by her close friend and colleague Henrietta Conrad (a very successful TV producer and founder of Princess Productions that she sold to Liz Murdoch's production empire), in Henrietta's London home.

Henrietta and Jemima are behind the latest American Crime Story TV series *Impeachment*, about the Monica Lewinsky–Clinton scandal. I wondered why Monica was at Jemima's a lot and now it all made sense. Anyhow, back to this particular party, which was packed and chaotic. Jeremy was very happy because Kristin Scott Thomas was there and I witnessed some serious flirting from him, which I found quite amusing.

He enjoyed that bit of the evening but was keen to get away as we became packed in like celebrity sardines. All of a sudden there was a great commotion as another few guests arrived. Jeremy and I were trying to squeeze out and the next thing I knew a rather pushy woman was herding a very young man through the hallway, and he couldn't help bumping in to me. He apologised profusely and continued to be dragged through the mêlée. He looked like a rabbit caught in the headlights as he was more or less thrown into an over-excited birthday girl and her fellow middle-aged party girls. I thought he looked a bit familiar, then Jeremy said, as we reached the front door, 'Did you see Harry Styles? I think he's Jemima's birthday treat.'

I was never quite sure how true that statement was. All I do know is that Harry is a very charming, polite young man who made an effort to come and apologise to me again, as Jeremy had a quick fag in the garden before we took a cab home.

*   *   *   *

Oh, what a night, just a pizza night …

Talking of Harry has reminded me of my favourite of all the Harrys. I was in the middle of planning logistics and accommodation for Clarkson, Hammond and May and their entourage for the European tour of *Top Gear Live* (pre-punch).

Jeremy called me late one morning and asked if I'd like to go to Hugh van Cutsem's fortieth birthday party in London. I hadn't originally been invited, as the van Cutsems were friends of Francie, Jeremy's ex-wife, but Rose, Hugh's wife, had spoken to Jeremy and insisted that I came.

I initially said I couldn't as I had so much to do before our imminent departure to Prague. Jeremy then texted me, saying, 'I know you don't care, but William and Kate are going to be there.' (That is Prince William and Kate.) With all due respect to the prince and his wife, no, I didn't care and I wasn't actually convinced they would be there anyway, as Jeremy had told me the party was at a pizza restaurant in Notting Hill and I really couldn't imagine the future king and his wife turning up there.

But Jeremy is quite persistent, as you might imagine; he does like to get his own way. He continued to text me. I decided that royalty or no royalty, it was more important that I honoured the invitation of the van Cutsems and their acceptance of me, the 'other woman'. So, as was so often the case, I organised last-minute childcare, worked a little faster and shot off to London.

To save time, I had arranged to meet Jeremy at Pizza East. No ordinary pizza restaurant, it's part of Nick Jones's Soho House group and is designed with the same cool, one-off interiors and serves the best pizza and other Italian delights using the finest ingredients.

The van Cutsems had taken over the top floor. As I arrived, I picked my way through the lowly, downstairs diners and climbed the stairs with a little anxiety as I was about to meet more key members of the Chipping Norton Set.

I was put at ease straight away, as the first person I saw was Jeremy, not far from the top of the stairs. He was chatting away to someone who had their back to me. I made a beeline for

Jezza then turned around to meet his bar companion, who was none other than Prince Harry. OMG! I had longed to give that boy and his brother, too, a huge hug for so long. I'd even had imaginary conversations with them, wanting desperately to relieve them of their grief and continuing struggles living their lives in the public eye without the love of their wonderful mother, whom I idolise.

In that moment, I simply greeted Harry as I would anyone else and was then completely mortified as Jeremy introduced me and said that I knew exactly what it felt like to be on the front pages and hounded by the press. I wanted the ground to swallow me up. How could Jeremy think my situation as the other woman to a high-profile motoring journalist, who was splashed across the papers now and again, was comparable to what Harry went through? Thank goodness Harry showed no objection to the comparison and general banter ensued. I was also saved any further embarrassment, as the staff had started urging us all to sit down.

Jeremy was seated at a table with Prince Harry in the middle of the restaurant and I was ushered around the corner to what looked like an 'overflow' table for those last-minute guests such as I was. I appeared to be the only one who was being led there, to an empty table. I persuaded the terribly pushy waitress to let me finish my drink at the bar and begged Jeremy to hang back with me.

Gradually a few more guests started to filter towards where I was seated in the dark corner of the 'odd table out'. I was soon joined by Martha Ward, fashion PR, whom I'd met on several occasions at Jemima Khan's and then by Alexander Armstrong, from the quiz show *Pointless*, whom I'd met at Jimmy Carr's.

We all settled in and started to joke that we were on the naughty table. Soon all the seats were taken and who should sit down right opposite me, just a pizza-restaurant-table's-width away from me, but Prince William.

OMGG!

I am tingling throughout my whole body remembering the moment. His good wife could not make it, but that certainly didn't dampen his spirits.

So, I can report that both princes are just exactly as you'd wish, but perhaps even better. William bantered away with us all. He very much reminded me of my younger brother and his friends, just a regular, witty, genuine guy.

Our 'naughty table' started to live up to its name when the birthday boy Hugh [van Cutsem] stood up to give a speech. Led by William, Hugh's childhood friend and neighbour in Sandringham, we all started heckling and complaining about having been put in the corner.

It was a great night. After dinner, the party continued and Jeremy, being the smoker that he is, ended up outside on the charming terrace tucked away at the back of the restaurant. It was the place to be; smokers are usually the best party animals. Unfortunately, with spirits running high, Jeremy, fuelled by plenty of rosé, let slip about a date he was set up on when he was actually having an affair with me, which, at the time, hardly anyone knew about, so people assumed he was a sad singleton going through a separation from his wife.

As you might imagine, I was a little upset and walked out, down the stairs and out of the restaurant. After some time spent wondering how to deal with what I'd just heard, I decided to go back in and not just leave the party, which would have been rude.

As I reached the top of the stairs, Prince Harry rushed towards me and said, 'He's looking for you, he's worried about you. I think he's gone back out onto the terrace.' OMFG! Could this night get any more surreal? Dear, dear, lovely Harry was so concerned about me and what had happened between Jeremy and me that he helped me to find the tart of a man that I had stupidly fallen in love with. At that point in the evening's proceedings, I would much rather have gone home with Harry and put the world to rights. Especially about the behaviour of some of the tabloid press.

*　*　*　*

Soon after my royal encounter, we set off, along with Hammond and May and all the *Top Gear Live* crew for the most intense and ambitious tour yet, departing just four days after we'd arrived back from Durban, South Africa. We did four cities in four different countries over ten days and the boys performed eight live arena shows during that time. It was pretty hectic, particularly if you add in some essential partying and sightseeing for the seemingly hyperactive presenters.

At the end of that intense run of shows, Jeremy was scheduled to fly from Turin to Morocco to film for *Top Gear*. We had had such a good time touring that he didn't want me to go home and asked me to join him in Morocco. I managed to change my flight at midnight the night before. There was never a dull moment sharing a life with Jeremy Clarkson.

I'd never been to Morocco, so that was another bonus. We had a very early flight after an end-of-tour party in Turin and, on arrival in Morocco, we were driven straight to the film location. Jeremy's work schedule was truly insane. Most of the time he loved it, but the strain was beginning to show. Every day there was at least one outburst from him. Something had to give.

He talked often of giving up his *Sun* column to free up some time and ease the pressure, but then he would do the maths and decide that it would pay for a couple of luxury holidays. He was also worrying about the costs of his divorce and of building the house of his dreams. And so his ridiculous timetable continued.

On location in Morocco, the crew had already been filming and Jeremy just needed to do a few pieces to camera. That is a speech directly to the camera, after one of his drives; in this instance he was proving just how amazing an old Peugeot Estate (and I mean old, it was a model from the seventies) was as a means of transport across the desert.

When we arrived, the classic Peugeot was parked at the bottom of the sand dunes and, to my surprise, an old friend, Charlie Butler-Henderson, jumped out of the car, taking off a mask as he did so. The mask was a face of Jeremy Clarkson. I had never known that Jeremy had stunt drivers. In all the time I'd been working with him, he'd never told me. Mind you, there was never time for a 'how was your day, dear' type of conversation. He was also very protective of the secrets of the trade.

It was strange to see my old friend Charlie, brother of Vicki, former *Top Gear* and now *Fifth Gear* presenter, with whom I'd worked for years on several car launches, dressed up as my boyfriend. Weird!!

It was great to watch Jeremy out on location, an extraordinary one at that, in the middle of the desert, looking across to the Atlas Mountains in the distance, with a camel and a Peugeot in the foreground.

Jeremy is a true pro and it didn't take him long to film his speeches, if with a little bit of moaning and groaning, before we headed back to our five-star hotel in Marrakesh, which proved to be yet another scene from a movie.

That was the upside of having a job in which you'd reached the top of your game and had the power to create a story wherever you wanted in the world, and had a team of dedicated people to set it all up and arrange everything you desired to make it happen. It was just a shame that there was so much work, and that it all happened at breakneck speed. Still, we were able to relax this time, around the pool, for a couple of hours, before getting changed for dinner.

There was hardly anyone staying in the resort. In fact, I think the majority of the guests were the *Top Gear* crew, but most of them were working until late into the evening, so Jeremy and I pretty much had the restaurant to ourselves.

I loved observing the different cultures around the world, as did Jeremy here in Morocco. It turned out to be quite an experience. The waiter, dressed in traditional costume and taking himself very seriously in his role, appeared at the table with a little more of a delay than we would have liked, considering there were literally only a couple of other diners.

Jeremy and I had already started to observe the behaviour of all the staff and amuse ourselves with their funny, inept ways. Us English, and especially people like Jeremy and me who have travelled extensively, expect tip-top service and can be terribly demanding. Tonight, we were clearly too much for this very slow and 'laid-back to the point of rudeness' type of service. It was as if they literally couldn't be bothered.

Jeremy and I started to guess how long they would take to come back with condiments and decided we should order our pudding whilst we were eating our starter so that we got it in time for bed. With plenty of alcohol to jolly us along, we were soon trying to contain our giggles at the *Fawlty Towers* experience we were having.

The most amusing thing by far was the fact that all the waiters would completely ignore me and would only address Jeremy. They didn't even bother to put things right when there was cutlery missing from my place setting; Jeremy made the request for me, but they delivered it without even looking at me, as if I wasn't even there. Whether it was a cultural thing about women in general we weren't sure. We decided that they didn't approve of me, Ms Sage, who was not Mrs Clarkson. Jeremy said: 'They probably think you are a whore!' in his best Harry Enfield voice.

That's one thing Jeremy and I were good at: having a laugh.

20

Farmer Clarkson

Away from the high life, we started to spend more time at the farm. We set up camp in the annexe of the original house. Once again, I was tasked with hoovering up swarms of dead flies and yards of spider webs. Once cleaned and equipped with staple equipment for the weekend, it resembled a student studio flat. Jeremy enjoyed just 'camping out' like this, as long as he had access to Lord and Lady Bamford's organic farm shop, which supplied his favourite rosé wine and 'brown food', as he called it, i.e., pies, sausages, beef, bread etc. Then he was very happy.

We had several low-key shooting parties with a few of the Chipping Norton Set and Jeremy even extended his generosity, which he rarely did, to the *Top Gear* crew, who, to their joy and amusement, were joined by Richard Hammond, who turned up in his Dakar Rally yellow Defender (Land Rover car), which of course Jeremy ripped into him about, just a tiny bit.

We were also joined by fellow farmer Alex James, who rocked up with a bottle of fine champagne. That was a bit awkward as Jezza was trying very hard not to drink.

With the help of Jeremy's family's resident handyman, we set up a huge fire in the nearly completely derelict farmyard and served up a breakfast of sausage and bacon rolls and a few sloe gin shots to set everyone up for the day.

Jeremy's sporadic attempts to give up alcohol were quite tricky and didn't put him in such a great mood. I was always blamed for putting the pressure on and ruining his life, which I took with good grace and humour in order to try to keep him on the right track. All was very jolly amongst the rest of the shooting party and we soon set out in our off-road convoy, including Jeremy's fully loaded Range Rover Autobiography, complete with bespoke drinks cabinet fitted in the boot, which at this time did rub the salt in Jeremy's wounds a little, however he did like showing it off.

Something which was unfortunately becoming more regularly apparent, especially when the big man was trying to remain sober, was his even shorter temper and lower tolerance level than usual. As we all exited the 4x4 vehicles and walked through the fields towards the first set of pegs (a peg is a spot allocated to each armed guest for the oncoming pheasant slaughter) one of the crew took a call on their mobile.

Jeremy snapped and bellowed at the poor girl to switch her phone off immediately. The big man was terrifying when he shouted angrily, especially when he was sporting a loaded shotgun. The party mood subsided and we all paid attention to his lordship's safety briefing, which of course was expected and to be respected, but it didn't need to be delivered as if by a dictator.

The shooting party quietly set off on foot to take up their positions, ready to take down the poor, unsuspecting pheasants. The relative silence was suddenly broken as the big man's phone went off. Looks were exchanged by the rest of the shoot, who had just shaken in their boots as only moments earlier they had been told, with no room for misunderstanding, that all phones should be on silent or off.

Of course, the man in charge is always right and his phone calls are way more important than anyone else's. Ironically, the crew were never off duty and the poor girl who had taken a call earlier was undoubtedly dealing with some future film-shoot logistics. This kind of unreasonable behaviour from Jeremy was happening more and more and was often a lot worse whilst he was not drinking. I imagined that having the temptation of a car-boot full of booze, and the finest crystal to serve it in, whilst enjoying his favourite sport didn't help his mood.

Jeremy and I would often fall out over such incidents, coupled with other relationship strains caused by his not only still being married, but also incredibly famous. He was also often in trouble for some offensive behaviour or other, so my tolerance was often stretched too far and I would tell the big man where to go, in no uncertain terms, only to be sweet-talked right back into his crazy world quite soon afterwards.

Despite his terrifying outbursts, the rest of us enjoyed the day's country pursuit and it all ended well in one of the Cotswolds's wonderful pubs, with an end-of-shoot dinner.

Jeremy and I had a lot of fun 'playing' at the farm, clearing paths, discovering streams, trees and plants, and messing about with Jeremy's numerous motorised toys. The seeds were definitely being sown for the launch of Farmer Clarkson.

He claimed his favourite day ever was a day we spent with two large tools (not James and Richard), two 'Kangos' I think they are called: giant, power hammer-drills, weapons of mass destruction for chipping away masonry. The pair of us took great satisfaction in drilling away, competing with each other to get the largest piece of render from the barns to hit the floor, exposing the beautiful Cotswold stone behind.

In true Chipping Norton style, though, there was always a party to attend, and although the focus on building a new life in the country was working well and the big man was really enjoying it, he couldn't miss the Brooks's summer party.

In a strange act of defiance, as if to make a point that he was trying to be a 'normal' person indulging in weekend DIY, he insisted on going to the party fresh from using his Kango, covered in masonry dust. To be fair, we didn't have any hot water at the farm and he said I could get a shower at Rebekah's house, but he was determined to stay in character as Bob the Builder, covered in demolition debris. I dared not criticise the new home-improvement guy. If anyone could get away with going to a high-society summer party looking as if he'd just survived Armageddon, Jeremy could.

*　*　*　*

Once the big deal with Amazon had been signed and sealed, it wasn't long before the retail giant started making the most of their new signing. Jeremy was asked to go out to Amazon's HQ in Seattle to film an advert for the new drones which were going to start delivering books, shoes or that 'essential household gadget' right to your door, or just outside it, in record time.

Jeremy is known for never wanting to be on his own, so as part of the deal I was to be flown out with him first class, and looked after as well, for the duration of the trip.

It was a pleasure to go on yet another extraordinary adventure. The Amazon people treated Jezza like some kind of god, which was a bit disconcerting as, to be honest, that's the last thing he needed, and when he was being his true self, that's the last thing he wanted either.

We were picked up on the first morning of filming by a limo and headed into downtown Seattle to a cool, refurbished brick warehouse. There was a huge crew of caterers with the finest healthy food – they'd been briefed that he was on a health kick.

There were lighting engineers, camera crew, hair, make-up and wardrobe.

The 'god' was greeted with too much enthusiasm and respect for my liking. I totally respected and admired Jeremy's professional abilities and incredible talent, but after the punch incident, those close to him were increasingly worried about the large number of sycophants surrounding him, enabling his bad behaviour and habits.

I'd always done a good job of bringing Jeremy back down to earth, but it was becoming increasingly difficult. He'd expressed his dislike of the huge amounts of fruit and salad that was laid out for lunch. One of the producers, anxious to keep him happy, asked me what he liked and offered various culinary delights, including fresh seafood, of which there was an abundance in Seattle. I informed them that he'd love a prawn cocktail – it was something that Hammond and May also loved, and I'd often arranged these for them whilst on tour.

Come lunchtime, enormous prawn cocktails were delivered to his private lounge area, accompanied by a huge platter of oysters. Keeping him grounded was going really well!!

As VIP guests of Amazon, and because Jeremy was filming to promote their drone delivery service, we were taken for an exclusive visit to the drone-development centre, which was in a top-secret location.

And I mean top secret. It even had a false entrance, which just looked like a typical industrial unit door, but once we were inside a further secret inner door was revealed with top security, for which we had to have special clearance and be accompanied by senior management.

Inside it was like being in Q's laboratory in a James Bond movie, where dozens of brainy IT geeks were beavering away amongst gadgets and high tech. In the centre of the building were two huge pens like large squash courts, with floor-to-roof-height, see-through walls. (I don't think they were glass as that wouldn't have worked given what went on inside the pens.)

These huge, empty pens turned out to be testing areas for the drones. It wasn't long before Jeremy got his hands on the remote controls.

I'd imagined the drones to be a similar size to camera drones, about one or two feet across, but these drones were way bigger, and these were just the prototypes. The ones that it was proposed would actually start filling our skies, were the length of a small car, looking like a cross between a biplane and a hydrofoil.

The technology was certainly very impressive. The idea was that if you subscribed to super-fast drone delivery, you would have a gadget that you placed on your front lawn or driveway that sent a signal to the drone directing it to the correct location.

This may well work in America in the suburbs, where there are large open spaces between each house and hardly any high fences or walls, but can you imagine drones ducking and diving through street upon street of terraced houses, with little or no gardens? Did Amazon imagine customers would lean out of their high-rise flat windows with the receiving gadget and wait to catch their order?

Of course I am not a scientist nor a flight engineer, and haven't thought through the technicalities of being able to carry a pair of trainers approximately fifteen miles a few hundred feet up in the air. If you Google 'Amazon drones' you will find his lordship performing with a bulldog to explain the proposed service.

Sadly, or perhaps not, the service has failed to get off the ground, literally; unlike Jeremy Clarkson and his two right-hand men on their *Grand Tour*.

We were further entertained by more senior management at one of the top restaurants in town, where it was rumoured that the King of Amazon, Jeff Bezos, was going to join us. I think he must have been behind with deliveries as he was a no-show.

His absence didn't spoil our fun, though, and Jeremy really enjoyed our evening with some fascinating heads of Amazon's cyber-security, two of whom had their own planetariums and telescopes out in the desert, keeping a close eye on any activity other than their drones in the sky, and beyond.

They shared their incredible photos of the universe way beyond Amazon, which Jeremy loved. He also enjoyed it when one of the PR team, in order to prove that although drones hadn't taken off, Amazon's express delivery certainly did work, ordered several items, like chocolate and Clarkson merchandise for us all. Very impressively, the delivery turned up before we'd finished pudding.

All that fun was had without the aid of alcohol for Jezza and he admitted that he had actually enjoyed the sober experience. He had now committed to not over-indulging in too much party activity until he had delivered the final live show at the O2 arena to end what had been an epic twelve years and more touring the world, mostly with the same crew, including me. It was definitely time to have a celebratory glass of something special to acknowledge the end of an epic *World Tour*.

21

Bollywood Bond

Jeremy had made it through three months of sobriety, which was highly commendable. At the end of the emotional final and incredible performance at the O2, which really was the end of the road of anything to do with the BBC and *Top Gear*, Jezza could not go without toasting that incredible achievement, and celebrating with his long-term colleagues with a glass of champagne.

Unfortunately, as I said earlier, one of Jeremy's friends once quoted, 'One drink is never enough, two is just right, three drinks are never enough!' The evening ended tragically with the big man blowing his top over another cold-food incident. I was devastated that my dream job and my dream relationship both appeared to be falling apart.

Throughout the turbulent, stressful last few years of our relationship, I had walked away many times. I was supported by many who were close to Jeremy and I travelled down a painful and very bumpy track with him. I'm not going to air our dirty laundry, but I did have to tell him to fu** off on numerous occasions for the sake of my own sanity.

At Christmas that year, we had a monumental break-up, as a result of which I cancelled an incredible trip to Mozambique:

a New Year holiday, though one which was partly intended as research for future Amazon films. As always happened, Jeremy begged me to go back to him, claiming he could not live without me.

At the start of one of our reunions, we had been invited to go to the Barbados estate of the Lloyd-Webbers. I was to meet Andrew and Madeleine, whom Jeremy had assured me I'd love, as Madeleine was seriously horsey, like me, and a lot of fun.

Our introduction was to be at an intimate affair: the engagement party of Rupert [Murdoch] and Jerry [Hall]. Not the bear and the mouse: the media mogul and the model.

I'm sure you've got the gist of this by now; Jezza does not do anything by halves, or quietly. His social life was no exception. I was actually seriously anxious about this event. Not only was I feeling fragile about our personal life, but to be meeting two of the most successful people in the world under the roof of one of the most powerful people in the world was quite daunting.

As we approached Mr Murdoch's residence in Mayfair, Jeremy commented, 'Well, there won't be any paparazzi here.' He was right. There were just some plain-clothed security chaps, who nodded politely as we passed.

Inside, it was absolutely packed. We quite quickly found Andrew and Madeleine Lloyd-Webber. I found it odd to be arranging to go on holiday with people I didn't know, and Jeremy didn't know them that well either. But Madeleine was lovely and we exchanged numbers in order to discuss any pre-holiday plans. She also very generously invited my son and any carer whom I wished to bring. She was very understanding of Alfie's specific needs as an autist. I was very touched.

We were kind of swept along with the crowds and moved into the next room and the balcony overlooking one of London's great parks. Adrian (Gill) and Nicola were there, which made me feel at home. Jeremy was most excited about who he might bump into and very much enjoyed bantering with Ed Vaizey, or should I say Baron Vaizey of Didcot, who was at the time the minister of Culture, Communications and Creative Industries. He was a real character, not dissimilar to Boris Johnson, seemingly just enjoying the job for the fun of it.

David and Samantha Cameron were there, albeit briefly. It was all very surreal, especially when I found myself chatting with Rebekah Brooks, who bizarrely asked me, 'Do you think it's going okay?' As if my humble opinion mattered!! I then came face to face with the bride-to-be, Miss Jerry Hall, who was shorter than I was, which surprised me, and who was accompanied by Dame Joan Collins, who immediately complimented me on my outfit, telling me how stylish I looked.

That was all I needed to float through life for evermore, never to worry about what I wore ever again. Clearly I have talent if the legend and ultimate style queen Joan tells me I'm stylish!?

After a quick chat with the Camerons and our holiday hosts the Lloyd-Webbers, we made our way out of the party of the century. What I thought strange was that at an engagement party, which is probably one of the most intimate moments of a couple's life, most of the guests were, let's say, various influential folk rather than the couple's nearest and dearest, and their oldest friends.

In actual fact, I had begun to realise that most of Jeremy's social life was about powerful, influential and very famous people, or all three rolled into one, and he did often say that he felt he had no actual friends he could just go down to the pub and have a laugh with, or discuss current woes with.

Tragically, one of the very few times he said he'd had such a great time was after his mother's funeral, when all his oldest friends, including Andy Wilman, who he was at school with and was part of his social life when he first came to London, came back to his flat in Holland Park to honour his mother and remember the good old days.

He told me it was like putting on an old pair of slippers. I loved watching him being so relaxed and having a laugh, reliving parties and general bad behaviour of their carefree youth together.

Sadly, Jeremy and I fell out yet again due to his drinking and general bad behaviour and I refused to go to Barbados with him to the Lloyd-Webbers. I apologised to Madeleine and to Andrew and they were very supportive. In fact, Madeleine said she totally understood, as she had experienced something similar to what I was going through with Jeremy and was very sympathetic to my cause.

She also left the invitation very much open; if I changed my mind, I could arrive at any time. But I stood my ground with the unruly big man and didn't go. However, while he was out there, he had lunch with the Bamfords, who also have an estate out in Barbados and had invited us both to their next big celebration in India for a joint seventieth birthday party, which would coincide with their wedding anniversary and JCB's seventieth anniversary. We had been officially invited some time before, but given the current state of play, I would not be joining Jeremy.

He had even written in his *Sun* column about a blow-out night he'd had whilst there and advised any young drinkers to save themselves before it was too late. It was quite tragic, really; he was obviously aware of his problem, but just couldn't deal with it.

Carole Bamford had other ideas and insisted that Jeremy should persuade me to join him at their big celebrations in India. He sent constant emails begging me, telling me Carole had said it would be such a shame if I missed out.

*   *   *   *

Yet again, I succumbed to Mr Clarkson's persuasive ways and promises of improvement. I also felt very honoured to be invited by the Bamfords and felt it would be rude not to go, as they had put so much on and were saving a place for me.

When I say they had put so much on, that is the understatement of the millennium. Part of Jeremy's charm offensive was that I had to see the invitation and itinerary pack, which was an exquisite work of art. Each personalised invitation was made from parchment more than likely from recycled paper and handmade, since the Bamfords are renowned for their belief in sustainability and for supporting local communities in their beloved India. Some were decorated with hand-stitching and pop-up scenes of Indian temples and intricately carved elephants. I have kept it all; each piece is a work of art.

Our journey began at Farnborough private airport, just one of the airports from which hundreds of guests were flown out in privately chartered planes. The planes' cabins were fitted with business-class seats throughout and Daylesford organic food and wine was served. Each seat had a white pillow, monogrammed with the occupant's initials – I still have mine. The flight alone was awesome, with fellow passengers such as my old friend Viscount Linley and his wife Serena; the Earl and Countess of Derby, who I was particularly interested in, firstly because they were very friendly, but more importantly because they owned a safari park – the stuff of my dreams! Rebekah and Charlie Brooks were on board, as were Alex and Claire James, the Lloyd-Webbers, and Alice B-B and Nick Love.

Despite all the guests coming from privileged backgrounds and having enjoyed most of the luxuries and delights of living in high society, all on board were very excited and marvelled at the luxury and the attention to detail which had gone in to planning the event. And this was just the very beginning of a five-day extravaganza.

* * * *

Day 1: On arrival at the Rambagh Palace Hotel, we were greeted by a ceremonial elephant, dressed in colourful robes and painted with floral decorations, all topped off by a stunning silver headpiece – oh, and a member of staff sitting atop in red robes and a turban. Other guests were put up at nearby luxury hotels, but we appeared to be in the number-one spot. We were led to our room and, yet again, I felt like I'd landed in a movie scene. The hotel was indeed a palace, the former home to the Maharaja of Jaipur.

As we settled in our room, we found more gifts from our most generous hosts. There were two beautiful boxes with books of Indian poetry, Daylesford bamboo socks, wraps, pashminas, traditional Indian necklaces, Bamford toiletries and delightful bracelets with silver Indian charms, which we were asked to wear to identify us to the hotel staff as guests of the Bamfords, which meant we could order anything and not pay for it.

We had tea served on our terrace overlooking the stunning gardens, where peacocks paraded about. Lunch was a relatively casual affair on the main terrace. It was a chance to share room-boasting stories with other guests, most of whom we knew, of course.

There was not much time to relax as there was shopping to be done. However, we didn't have to venture out. The Bamfords had arranged for their favourite Indian vendors to come to us. They had set up an Indian Bazaar on the lawns of the palace hotel. Also on hand were tailors to make any alterations, and hair accessories and bindis were available.

We had four evening dinners and events to attend, so the bazaar was perfect for any wardrobe crisis or if any additional components were required.

The first evening was described as a welcome dinner, a garden party. We assumed it would be quite a casual affair, but it soon became apparent that nothing was going to be casual over the next few days. We were greeted with flower garlands and champagne; there was a tiny hint of casualness in that the food was a buffet and you could sit where you chose, but the tables were dressed in white linen and there were candles and flowers galore. After a welcome speech, the pièce de résistance for the evening was the Indian Mounted Army – let's call them that, though I'm sure there's a far more glamorous name for them. More than twenty horses and soldiers paraded along the edge of the gardens and stood on ceremony. The flag-bearing, turban-wearing soldiers looked quite magical astride their gleaming white, Marwari horses from Rajasthan, which have unique turned-in ears with bent tops.

Jeremy was on his best behaviour, drinking only lightly. He said this was to be his last hurrah before he focused on giving up for good. We, right out of character, went for an early night, partly in preparation for the activities and party planned for the next day, and partly due to travel and heat exhaustion. India is HOT.

* * * *

Day 2: Yoga – optional – not one for Jezza. (Although he has been known to dabble in Pilates, with Charlie Brooks, when both in their respective London residences. I had a strong suspicion, though, that they just lay watching their female instructor stretching her body.)

We had been offered four alternative activities for the day which we had been asked to book in advance. We'd opted for the city tour exploring temples and shops. Some of the ladies went all out and had full saris made for them for the final big night. Jeremy bought me a canvas bag with a car on it!! (I love it. It has one of those classic fifties Indian sedan cars, an Ambassador I think, in sparkly pink as a central motif.) We then joined the rest of the guests for a special lunch at the City Palace, the private residence of the royal family of Jaipur.

At the palace we were greeted by more dressed-up elephants and a welcoming traditional Indian band. As we entered, we were showered with flower petals and led through to the inner courtyard to be met by local dignitaries and possibly the royal family. I can't actually remember as it was all rather overwhelming and there were hundreds of us. It was a wonderful experience, but still very much a gentle warm-up for what was to come.

That evening's entertainment was to start at one of the other stunning hotels a few miles away. We were told it would be an Indian street bazaar. Once again, I had severely underestimated what we were about to experience.

We had been instructed to dress up in Indian costume for the evening and were offered clothes from a specially arranged dressing-up box at the Rambagh Palace Hotel. Jeremy is not one for fancy dress, but he did don one of his silk jackets from a previous Asian adventure.

Upon arrival at yet another stunning venue, we were served Indian canapés and more champagne. Then something quite extraordinary happened. Lord and Lady Bamford were taken in some kind of ornate, ceremonial carriage and we were instructed to follow on foot. As we reached what I thought was the boundary of the hotel gardens we were led through a gate to be greeted with what felt like a mile or more of street performers, musicians, more dressed-up elephants and horses. It was truly mind-blowing and actually quite an emotional experience as we meandered along the magical lantern-lit pathway surrounded by Indian delights.

We eventually arrived in the beautiful courtyard of a kind of folly. The whole place had been decorated and there were dozens of street-food vendors. The party's pace was picking up. It became like an Ibizan hedonistic club night, Indian style, complete with hubbly-bubbly pipes, which Jeremy and I quite enjoyed in the ornate chill-out inner courtyard scattered with large cushions and rugs. We hubbled and bubbled around a fire pit guarded by ornate elephant statues.

It was a truly magical evening, unfortunately slightly marred by Alex James getting naked on the bus back to our hotel! Now that's rock 'n' roll.

* * * *

Day 3: This was a busy day. After breakfast, all guests were loaded onto coaches, something which ordinarily Jeremy would have hated, but when the coach is full of lords, ladies, rock-'n'-roll stars and millionaires it is bearable.

It was quite a long trip to our next event, another thing viewed with disfavour by chain-smoking Jezza, but with the aid of nicotine gum, which he chewed like a masticating cow on speed, he survived. In the meantime, I enjoyed the incredible sights of India, including a funeral procession with the old man who had passed laid out for all to see on a makeshift stretcher, surrounded by marigold flowers and carried high by, I assume, his family members.

We passed hundreds of street sellers selling pretty much anything to scrape by. I have no idea how they did make money as so often their stalls, which were crammed in next to each other, all appeared to be selling the same things.

India is chaotic, dirty, colourful, incredibly spiritual, beautiful and engulfed in poverty, so to go from palace to palace and then arrive at what appeared to be a brand spanking new and shiny 'JCB Town' felt a little uncomfortable. Although I have to say that the Bamfords support the country as a whole by generating many jobs and they are renowned for looking after their staff well.

JCB started operations, introducing heavy machinery and excavators into India, in 1979. Since then they have gone on to employ over 10,000 people in their factories and dealerships. This latest facility was a state-of-the-art eco-friendly manufacturing plant.

The Bamford family also run charities and foundations in India, supporting artisan crafts and trades, helping to train the next generation. One of them is Nila House, which produces beautiful homeware and clothing, all hand-crafted and made very much with the planet and the people of India in mind. The Daylesford shops, both in London and Gloucestershire, on the edge of the Cotswolds, stock the Indian delights which Lady Bamford carefully selects. She lives, breathes and wears all the products herself.

Sorry, I've gone a bit off track. We arrived at the latest JCB factory, which, for this special day celebrating seventy years of JCB, had been transformed into an Indian festival. We entered under a JCB arch, two diggers strategically placed with their back hoes (I think that's the correct term) raised at full stretch, meeting in the middle and decorated with flowers.

A red carpet was laid for hundreds of metres, the full width of the main building; flags of united nations were flying at full mast; there were decorative urns with hundreds of marigolds spilling out of them (marigolds are a traditional Indian flower which represents sun and positivity – there were plenty of both of those wherever we went!); there were drummers drumming; and dancers dancing in full costume. The whole scene was an explosion of colour, affecting all your senses, and this went on for the whole length of the red carpet which led us to a village of marquees providing food and drinks. There were camels, tumbling dwarfs, a whole circus of performers, and of course the majestic and wonderful fully decorated elephants.

We honoured guests milled around, aghast yet again at what had been created for these very special celebrations. And so, the spectacles continued. After pre-lunch champers to top up our hangovers, we were guided through to the factory. The entrance foyer had an incredible floor, an art installation of coloured rice laid out to form a stunning floral motif. God knows how many painstaking hours it had taken to create. It would have been like attempting a million-piece puzzle. And yes, somebody did accidently walk through it!

We arrived in a huge warehouse which had been transformed into a dining area for a gala lunch, a talk and films on the history and success of JCB, from its humble beginnings in Uttoxeter, Staffordshire, England, where Joseph Cyril Bamford, our host's father, created the first tipping trailer from war-surplus materials. The rest, as they say, is history. JCB has obviously gone on to be a hugely successful global brand.

After lunch and more entertainment, a huge temporary curtain that we all thought was there just to create a wall for the dining area, was dropped as what I would call reverse-fireworks rained down like a waterfall of light, revealing the uniformed JCB workforce and a huge display of the latest diggers, equipment and machinery, along with more floral rice motifs to make it all look pretty. We then had a chance to climb all over 'everyone's favourite diggers' and take silly photos of ourselves lying in giant scoops or pretending to drive the glorious machines. And I've just remembered the table favours were toy JCBs, which I loaded up on as my boy is a big fan.

Could things get any better? Yes! We were loaded back onto our coaches and driven off to the airport to take another first-class trip to the lakes of Udaipur. We boarded our jet with the same passengers we'd flown out with. Spirits were high, as you might imagine, and we were all bonding on this most magnificent of all holidays.

Alas, nothing is ever perfect, even for billionaires; even they can't control everything. There was a major issue with air-traffic control or some other aviation body and we were held on the runway for hours, then yet more hours. Of course, there was plenty of delicious organic Daylesford food and wine, but only a limited supply. We honourable guests were suddenly overcome with anxiety. Would we end up starving and ending our days on a luxury private jet?

No. Eventually, we were allowed to take off, even though we were dangerously low on supplies of refreshments, but we made it to our next stunning destination, albeit about ten hours late. We were informed that the party and dinner planned for the evening would still go ahead despite the terrible delay. But for all the incredible hospitality and comfort we had been afforded, the reality was that most of us were exhausted. After much debate, our inner circle of fellow partygoers decided we had to put our best party feet forward and soldier on.

Our hotel suite was exquisite, which immediately lifted our weary spirits and provided ample motivation for us to get showered and changed for the next event. All the hotels for the Bamfords' guests were set around the main lake of Udaipur and we had to get water taxis, which took us, of course, to another beautiful island palace hotel.

Every guest who made it was soon re-energised as yet again an incredible feast was laid before us in beautiful surroundings. It was quite a casual affair compared with the events so far, but by no means disappointing in any way. Jeremy and I left when the youngsters amongst us started dancing on the tables. Neither of us likes to miss out, but our age was starting to catch up with us, that and the low alcohol consumption rule that Jezza had in place.

Back in our exquisite room, which opened out onto a private garden overlooking the lake and temples beyond, we relaxed. The garden was a mini-paradise, formed of small lakes decorated with waterlilies and framed by palms and other tropical foliage. Just outside the room was a plunge pool, from where decking paths led to a small terrace with a swing chair, where we chose to end another extravagant evening with a nightcap.

The night was not quite so idyllic. I couldn't sleep because of the noise of the frogs, which I loved, but the sound was just too intrusive for my ears. I had also started to feel the ominous rumbles of Delhi belly.

The sun rose early and so did I, with a need to get to the loo as quickly as possible. I was gutted, literally, but determined to soldier on, as I had planned to go riding with my new best friend Lord Linley and a few others. I was determined not to miss the opportunity to experience the extraordinary rare-breed Marwari Rajasthan horses with their funny little ears and unique gait.

I braved it to breakfast and sat with Christopher Biggins and his delightful partner Neil. The breakfast gossip was that many were being struck down by dodgy tummies. I managed a bite or two of dry toast then felt the urgent need to get back to our room and take some more Imodium. With regret, I had to pull out of my riding adventure.

* * * *

Later that morning, armed with Imodium and loo roll, Jeremy and I headed out on the lake to visit the Lloyd-Webbers for lunch at the Taj Lake Palace Hotel, the very famous hotel that was featured in the James Bond movie *Octopussy*, starring Roger Moore. (I wonder if he got Delhi belly? If he did, I bet Q had a gadget to deal with it.)

I didn't eat anything other than a few chips. The discussion turned to the shenanigans of the night before; apparently, Alex James got naked again and was found on the lawn of their hotel.

Us girls, including Madeleine, discussed our outfits for the grand finale of celebrations later that evening. She invited me to join her in the hotel shop to look at the jewellery, suggesting Jeremy could treat me to something. The jewellery was not just jewellery of the sort you might find on your average high street in Ernest Jones, it was more like viewing the crown jewels! Madeleine decided on her pieces, for which Andrew willingly parted with a few thousands to buy. Jezza, however, was not going to allow his true Yorkshireman self to be conned into buying something that was clearly overpriced. Jeremy and I continued our day, taking a boat to the mainland to explore the historic buildings and shops. Jeremy promised to buy me something there, to complement my outfit for the main event that evening.

In a small shop, crammed with jewels with price tags of hundreds rather than thousands of pounds, which were actually more to my taste in artisan silver, we were given a warm Indian welcome and had coffee made for us whilst I perused the hundreds of necklaces, rings and bangles. Before the big man ran out of patience, I chose a beautiful necklace, earrings, bracelets and anklets in traditional Indian-style silver. We were both happy, especially Jezza, who felt he'd got far more for his money, and that I would be suitably decorated.

After a quick dash around a castle or palace – I can't quite remember the detail – it was time to get a boat back to start preparing for the evening event. And what an event that was to be. Never in my wildest dreams could I have imagined anything like what we were about to experience.

Jeremy might not like fancy dress, but he did enjoy dressing up on this occasion. It was a themed evening called a Raj White Night, and yet another beautiful hand-crafted invitation which could have doubled as an ornament had arrived in our room that morning. We already knew that we all had to dress in white. Jeremy had dug out his white tuxedo and with his tan he actually looked quite handsome.

We met Bryan Ferry, as you do, in the bar for a quick pre-event G and T and then headed to board our scheduled boat which took us to the venue for the evening, Jagmandir Island, which also featured in *Octopussy*. It's a tiny island, apparently usually home to a very small hotel with just seven hideaway suites, but on this night of all nights it had been dressed by an incredible event team with what must have been a pretty open-ended budget. The whole island had been completely taken over by Lord and Lady Bamford.

As we cruised across the lake we could see the stunning location lit up like Disneyland. Each temple-like area was beautifully lit with lanterns and full-colour stage lighting.

The evening began with champagne on the lawns looking out to the lake. Everyone looked stunning, except Nick Love, who was wearing spotted pyjamas, probably silk, knowing Nick, but definitely pyjamas. His style was as cheeky and as loveable as he was. The rest of the guests had gone for full Bollywood White Night glamour. Lord and Lady Bamford looked like Indian royalty, which they kind of are out there.

The Derbys also looked like royalty. They had borrowed their stunning bejewelled outfits from friends at home who had just attended an Indian wedding. They were the real deal. The whole scene was fit for a modern-day Bond film, including the explosions. Thankfully not killer ones, but of a huge firework display over the water, a display to match any city's New Year celebrations, with the added attraction of water fountains, lit up in ever-changing colours, synchronised with music.

We were then led past more elephants, just sculptures, and floral displays with literally thousands of flowers, lit by hundreds of candles and lanterns which decorated the entrance to an inner courtyard which had been transformed into the most beautiful dining area you can imagine, and then imagine some more.

The scene was mesmerising: long tables dressed with white linen, white flowers and candles running in an unbroken line down the centre, complemented by white floral standard trees and the palm trees which grew naturally in the courtyard. The lighting was incredible. Somehow, modern chandeliers had been suspended above the tables, even though above us was only sky! The Bamfords had certainly reached for the sky and beyond with this celebratory bash.

The entertainment was incredible, too. Several musicians and singers performing different genres of music moved among us, and even on the tables, whilst we ate. The excitement was palpable, especially when the Prince of Greece got up on our table and danced, arms outstretched, whilst balancing his drink on his head! Even Clarkson was up on his chair. The atmosphere was more than electric.

After dinner, the dancing moved to the dance-floor, complete with podiums, on one of which I ended up dancing with the then editor of the *Daily Mail*, Geordie Greig. Jeremy commended me, saying it should help to keep me off the front pages. It didn't. The evening was filled with yet more didn't-see-that-coming moments, including supplying drugs to Viscount Linley – no, not those sorts of drugs, the essential Indian trip drug, Imodium. However, it did provide a great scene of David and me huddling over my clutch bag, searching for the life-saving pills.

We were further entertained by a mash-up of a rock band comprising Nick Mason (Pink Floyd) on drums, Alex James (Blur, and not naked this evening) on bass guitar, with lead singer, guitar and keyboards talentedly executed by one of Jezza's favourites, Steve Winwood.

Now that is rock 'n' roll, Bollywood, Hollywood and Bond all rolled into one!

Carole was right; it would have been a great shame to have missed it. Thank you, Lord and Lady B.

As my sister-in-law once said, you may not have had the wedding, but you have certainly had a good few honeymoons. The best part of that particular Indian honeymoon was that Jeremy had learnt that the best part of a party is the beginning, when everyone's excited and the alcohol buzz hits you; things then reach a crescendo before they start, finally, to get messy and that, he decided, was the time to leave.

Perhaps we were making progress towards a more sedate life?

Er, no. Next stop: Jordan.

22

Supper Fit for a King

Yes, we were airborne again, but this time for work. It was the first big film for Amazon and I had been employed to help look after the boys on location, just like my job with the *Top Gear Live* tour, i.e., make sure they had anything they needed, whether food, drink, medication or clothing. I literally had to follow them around with a bag of things they might just want or need.

The adventure began as soon as we boarded the plane. Up front, in the seats with more leg room was someone who doesn't need it, ironically, but he had the money and definitely the contacts to get him any seat around the world. It was Matthew Freud.

Matthew spotted Jeremy straight away and it was arranged that we should join him for dinner at his friend's house. His friend was the King of Jordan. James and Richard would be left out, which I thought was a bit mean, and I felt rather awkward because I was supposed to be looking after them too. However, they were used to getting snubbed by the big man and politely and humbly accepted going straight to our hotel. They did have Gav, our ex-SBS security guard, to watch over them and he was also capable of rustling up emergency cigarettes etc. James and Richard also enjoyed just a quiet beer in a bar, rather than anything fancy.

So, upon arrival in Jordan and expecting to have to go through passport control, Matthew ushered us to one side, where we were waved on and met by human mountains – the king's men. Rather abruptly I was stopped by a giant hand held up rather menacingly in front of me. Apparently when Matthew put the call in to his highness to put more potatoes on, he hadn't mentioned me.

Feeling rather violated and alarmed, I said to Jeremy, who was all flustered, 'Don't worry, I'll go with the others.' Jezza was actually quite a gent and said, 'No, if you're not going, I'm not.'

Wow! That was a moment. Matthew, being the PR guru that he is, soon had it all sorted and the man mountain bowed his head and waved me on.

I was feeling a little on edge, and not very welcome, but there was no time to worry as we were whisked at high speed in the royal security convoy that had clearance through any traffic lights or traffic hold-ups. I had a sense of what it might feel like to be kidnapped as our armed guards sped us to the palace.

I say palace, but after our incredible Indian adventure it looked to me more like an up-market holiday complex with high security. Upon arrival, security seemed to soften, perhaps because we were back within the safety of the palace walls.

We were led by palace staff with Matthew into his private apartment for a drink and to wait to be told the king was ready to see us. Eventually Matthew got a call and he led us past an indoor pool and terrace area, through a large lounge area into a small side room, like a private members' bar of a nightclub.

We sat discussing the paraphernalia on the walls, which included ancient weaponry. This unnerved me slightly, but I settled in to nibbling on the snacks at the bar. Matthew then told us we might be joined by another palace guest, Bono.

Of course, Bono! That is exactly who you'd expect to meet in a Jordanian palace!? This was obviously going to be just an ordinary quiet late-night gathering with the King of Jordan, Jeremy Clarkson, Bono, Matthew Freud and me. Quite ordinary.

We continued observing our surroundings until an ordinary chap in a polo shirt appeared, said good evening and offered us drinks. Naturally he asked me, the only lady, first. 'I'll have a gin and tonic, please. Thank you.' When he turned away to get pouring, Jeremy nudged me and whispered, 'That's the king.' OMFG, you really couldn't make it up, especially when Bono then joined us and the four giants of showbiz and world peace were together to discuss how to change the world. I was left quietly observing and listening, sipping my G and T.

Apart from mixing a good alcoholic beverage, the King of Jordan gave me hope that the world could be changed for the better. Despite not recognising him, even though I had undoubtedly seen him on the news at some point, in yet another bizarre six-degrees scenario, a friend of mine and auntie to my boy, Marian (my boy's father's sister), had actually worked directly for the king and his good wife Queen Rania, running their personal affairs and the palace, in which I found myself standing.

Marian had told me they were the nicest king and queen she'd worked for – she had actually worked for a few, especially in the Middle East. She spoke of the good work he did, and he was just affirming that. I was going to go into detail, but I may not get my facts straight and I don't want to breach Jordanian and, worse yet, international security. God, how did I end up there!!

Jeremy felt the same. Even though he was no stranger to meeting people in high places and being a special guest, what was endearing was that it seemed he found it as exciting as I did.

So, yet another late night and an early start for the first day of filming with the boys.

*   *   *   *

Part of the discussion the night before had been that the location for filming was the king's very own state-of-the-art King Abdullah II Special Operations Training Center for the elite forces to perfect their skills against terrorists. The king had offered his butler's number to me in case we needed anything.

Despite the reassurance of the relationship we now had with 'the boss' – King Abdullah is the supreme commander of the Jordanian armed forces – it was pretty daunting arriving at the armed gate for our passports and pre-booked passes to be checked to allow access to the huge training camp, set in what appeared to be a vast, disused quarry, complete with runway and decommissioned plane to play with. The facility could accommodate over 1,000 soldiers at any one time, providing them with medical care, a state-of-the-art gym, an equipment and clothing store, a running track and a football pitch.

I was very excited, but not well prepared. My All Stars (shoes) were not army issue and I became incredibly lame very quickly as I was running around on the rough, rocky terrain for the three amigos. Clearly, I would have failed at the first training session.

One of our ex-SBS security guys escorted me to the kit shop and I bought super army socks as I called them (extra thick) and some proper desert boots. Meanwhile, the boys were about to get fully dressed up as Super Army Soldiers, as Jeremy named them. One of the young crew had raided the army surplus and got three of everything and spares to kit out the boys. You will have seen the episode if you're a fan. I can tell you that there was little acting required when it came to the men enjoying being soldiers for the day and pretending to shoot each other.

They were long and hard days in searing heat. Jeremy would lose his patience with James, and Richard would get fed up with being ridiculed for being short. James would be slow and stubborn. Situation normal. At one point I was asked by one of the producers to see if I could get Jeremy to be a bit more tolerant of James. That was one of the ridiculous and tricky challenges I faced in my bizarre job.

Jeremy is a perfectionist when it comes to filming and he pushes everyone and everything to the limit, including himself. If you haven't seen this particular Amazon episode, you should. He actually descends from a Chinook helicopter by abseiling, not one of his usual pastimes. And, as he kept reminding us, it was a very brave one at that. Or stupid – you decide. He also forced himself through a window way too small for him to fit through and had his testicles shot at. He defies medical science, fuelled by alcohol and fags as he is, rather than fruit and veg. I do not know how he is still functioning.

There was a lot of shouting, moaning and laughter, but the pressure was full-on, the background crew working harder than anyone. The result was an epic episode, one of the first on Amazon. I should have got a credit as I was involved in the spontaneous make-up team, creating a blown-up version of Jeremy Clarkson, smearing theatrical blood and charcoal all over his face, hair and chest. I also helped James's hair look the part after he'd supposedly been electrocuted whilst trying to hotwire a lorry. Something else to add to my rather eclectic CV.

* * * *

My logistical achievements for the flight home I will not be adding to my CV. This was my first official job looking after the boys on location with Amazon and part of my job was ensuring their travel logistics went as smoothly as possible. The production office booked all the flights and cars to and from the boys' homes. I had all the flight details, drivers' details and tickets to be handed out as and when.

I had to organise a mini-bus taxi to take us to the airport for our departure. I'd discussed with Gav, the security guy who would be travelling with us, what time we should leave the hotel. It was an early-morning flight and we were assured by the hotel staff and driver that there would be no traffic.

Jeremy would always question airport transfer arrangements as one of his pet hates was getting to airports too early and hanging around where he couldn't smoke and would undoubtedly be harassed by fans. The night before departure after another late finish Clarkson, Hammond and May were in the bar starting to wind down although there was still work being done, and perfectionist Jezza was demanding to see the rushes (the unedited versions of the films produced that day).

I tentatively informed them of the plan for the morning and the suggested departure time, which was around 6.30 a.m. They all moaned, especially the big man, who queried the distance to the airport, flight time etc. before deciding that we didn't need to leave till 7 a.m. at the earliest.

Morning arrived and we assembled as planned in the hotel foyer, last-minute fags were being drawn out for as long as possible. Eventually, we set off. There was no traffic on the road, all was perfect. We arrived at the relatively small airport, which was completely empty apart from the security staff, of which there were an extra layer that we had to endure to gain any access at all.

The place was deserted. Worryingly so. We headed to the BA desks. There was not a soul to be seen. I ran back to the entrance security and spoke my finest, slowest English, hoping they would understand. The clock was ticking, the fuse was shortening on Mr Clarkson. I couldn't find anyone who knew what was going on.

Tempers were frayed. I was terrified we were going to miss our flight, which was looking more and more likely. At last we found a ground-crew member who explained that Jordan's airport has a policy of a much earlier closing time at the check-in desk, different from any other airport in the world. Oh, fu**, the first foreign trip managing Amazon's budget and I had messed up big time. It was one of those things which I should have checked and checked again, but I had been complacent. In my defence, the mistake was at least partly because the big man always knows best and had to have the last word.

That was the big mistake that Gav and I both felt responsible for, not pushing back on the big man to allow that all-important extra time in the event of unforeseen delays, let alone ridiculous efficiencies and weird rules.

I suddenly remembered that the king had given me the number of one of his key staff whom he'd said I could call if I needed anything. Despite blowing the budget, I had just redeemed myself a little. Richard, who went off uncomplainingly to book five more flights, managed to get us all on the next flight out with his shiny new business credit card. He was feeling quite pleased with himself for having been able to solve a problem without the help of the kind of full entourage he was so used to with *Top Gear Live* and the BBC.

I had managed to secure VVIP treatment with the help of the royal butler and we were whisked through to the royal departure lounge for some good Jordanian hospitality before finally returning home. Mission complete.

* * * *

Back home we were getting really excited about the cottage we were renovating for us to have a base at the farm in order to start on the much bigger project of the main house, which we would eventually move into. That would have an orangery, a huge kitchen and living area, a grand dining area and a carefully positioned office for the main man, as well as a basement to incorporate a cinema room and, undoubtedly, a wine cellar! We both enjoyed sketching out room plans, especially for our bedroom suite with a huge bathroom, with bath strategically placed to take in the expansive view.

Jeremy would knock the socks off design expert Kevin McCloud. He loved thinking of every detail and was insistent on not having loads of ridiculous electrical gadgets and switches. He had learnt from the mind-bending experience of having a flat in London with all of that. There was always something going wrong and you'd have the curtains stuck open, or closed, whichever way you didn't want them, or annoying alarms going off because a spider had walked past a sensor. One thing that really annoyed him was that he could never work out the sound system. There was either no music, or music in the bedroom when you wanted it in the living room. For all its so called modern convenience, it was a good old-fashioned pain in the arse!

We enjoyed walks and quad-bike safaris over the 1,000 acres that the big man had taken under his wing, ready to become Farmer Clarkson. He loved the wild flowers, of which there were some incredibly rare ones that flower-spotters came from miles away to see. That, he didn't like, and I had to stop him from shouting, 'Get off my land!' on several occasions. I was very concerned about the fact that there was a public footpath running right up the driveway and past the door of the cottage and the entrance to the proposed manor. I didn't relish the thought of Clarksonesque run-ins with local ramblers in the future. That hadn't gone very well at his home on the Isle of Man. Meanwhile we were focused on the cottage, which was going to be our interim country retreat. To be honest, I would have been quite happy in that. Jeremy knew that and always laughed at me and how easily I was pleased. It was big enough, there were two separate ends to it, so Alfie, my boy, could pretty much have had his own wing and Jeremy and I could have had a grown-up living area made out of the old courtyard. However, it would never have been big enough for serious entertaining, which, of course, was high on his list.

Jeremy was quite daunted by getting the main house built and he discussed this with his two favourite girlfriends, Jemima and Sunetra, who had managed to oversee huge building projects as well as work and enjoy a busy social life. I love that kind of project and it was basically what I'd done for most of my working life, project manage. I was having good practice on the cottage, meeting up with the builders and the 'bat man'. The whole farm had to be inspected for bats, who basically have right of way over humans – I wonder if that law has changed since blooming Covid! Although, of course, we still don't know exactly where the disease originated. Jeremy was not best pleased about any restrictions or red tape that had to be fought through before you as much as mixed up some cement.

His love of interior design became very evident and we enjoyed shopping for new sofas for the upgraded penthouse and starting to collect homeware for the cottage, choosing fabrics and carpets. It was fun … until it wasn't!

I would do a bit of research in John Lewis and in the pages of *Homes & Gardens* and the like and then we would do targeted shopping in Jeremy's favourite shops: Peter Jones in Chelsea and The White Company.

Jeremy loves Peter Jones, a retail relative of John Lewis – they're basically the same shop. He claimed they have everything you could possibly need in your house, and it was all good quality.

However, as I've said before, it is not easy undertaking such a simple task as shopping with the very famous Jeremy Clarkson, who is constantly spotted. It's like shopping with an unexploded bomb which feels as if it's going to blow at any minute, just from the expectation of hassle from fans. He locks on to what he wants and moves at high speed to, say, the curtain section, flicks through them and makes an incredibly quick decision with no discussion on possible options. If I was lucky, and if the shop was quiet, he might move at a slower pace and allow me to have an opinion.

We had a ridiculous argument over a small kitchen utensil which he declared was the best one and that was when, as the more experienced cook, I dared to suggest otherwise. I was accused of causing arguments about everything. Then I knew it was getting close to wine o'clock. We piled up our haul at a cash desk and arranged for it to be ready for collection after a swift glass or two of rosé.

Jeremy's way of tackling Christmas shopping was to meet up with Sunetra Atkinson in Selfridges, have lunch, get pissed, then go around with his girly advisor and pick things off that were gathered together by a VIP service for him to pay for in one go at the end. Although I used to get pissed off with him for getting stupidly drunk, I did quite well out of those trips and I was very grateful to Sunetra for her input, and Selfridges for their brilliant, quality ranges.

23

Birthday Boy

With all the ups and downs over the years around Jeremy's separation from his wife and losing *Top Gear* he had not had very jolly birthdays – apart from one in Mustique that wasn't bad. With things getting a little more settled, I had arranged a surprise dinner with the help of Tony and Rita Gallagher, now Sir Tony and Lady Rita, courtesy of good old Boris. Tony had offered us on numerous occasions one of their cottages to stay in whilst we were working on the cottage and farm.

We were checking over the latest building works and making decisions on where to place appliances etc. when I told him I'd booked somewhere for dinner, an early one, and a night in a hotel instead of the fly-infested annexe.

As we drove out for the evening, I directed him towards Tony's vast estate and told him this was our 'hotel' for the night and I'd invited a few friends for dinner. Tony was his usual generous self and had offered me full use of his butler, who had helped arrange for a grand piano to be placed in the orangery to be revealed along with the incredible singer, who at that time went by the name of Lily Sastry, daughter of Rowan Atkinson and Sunetra Sastry.

Our dinner guests were David and Samantha Cameron, Rebekah and Charlie Brooks, Alex and Claire James, Sunetra Sastry and Dom Collins, Jeremy's best Chipping Norton buddy. I'd sent out invitations with the tongue-in-cheek dress code of: worn-out Levis, open-necked shirt, jacket and loafers for the gents, and party wear for the ladies.

Jeremy and I settled in to one of Tony's five-star-and-beyond cottages complete with huge wide-screen TV for watching the Grand Prix with a hangover, kitchen, enormous dining table and beautiful bedroom and bathroom.

The party began in one of Tony and Rita's grand reception rooms, and I mean grand – think Buckingham Palace. Once I knew all the guests had arrived, I led Jeremy in. He loved it. Some of his best Chipping Norton allies were there to cheer him on his big day, having survived a few years going through his divorce and all.

The best-dressed guest was Charlie Brooks. He'd nailed it, wearing jeans, open shirt stuffed with a cushion, casual jacket and loafers, topped off with a cardboard Clarkson mask. He'd even coincidentally got the same coloured shirt and jacket on as Jeremy had that night. I have the best picture of our then prime minister, Dave, in between Jeremy Clarkson and his rather short, twin brother, Charlie.

The evening was a great success with a lot of laughs, great entertainment, including jamming with Alex, who had brought his guitar, and sexy Lily's fab version of Marilyn Monroe's 'Happy Birthday'. The only low points were a drunken speech from me and me telling the PM to put his phone away at the dinner table! Oh, and the owl birthday cake I'd made for the birthday boy. I don't think the Gallaghers' highly qualified chef knew what to make of it, but my cake was dutifully and respectfully cut up and served. Ooh, and I've just remembered I may have been stroking the prime minister's arm and said, 'You have hardly any hair, your skin is so smooth.' I really didn't see that coming and I don't think Mr Cameron had either, but he did seem to enjoy the attention.

*   *   *   *

Jeremy loves his music and was regularly invited as a special guest to many concerts. On tour he was nicknamed 'the rockasaurus' as he knew so many artists, tracks, lyrics and the history of the bands and their members. The producer of the live shows, who had worked with him for years said there was no point in getting into an argument with him as he knew everything about anything. I guess you'd expect nothing less from someone with such a large head!?

He opened my mind and ears to many music genres that I would never have bothered with or hadn't even heard about before. One of those ear-bending experiences was to see and hear legendary guitarist Wilko Johnson play with Roger Daltrey at the Hammersmith Palais.

I had never heard *of* Wilko, but I almost certainly had heard *him*. He played for many well-known bands, providing his unique and amazing guitar techniques. He was a member of the rock/rhythm-and-blues band Dr Feelgood, has worked with Ian Dury and the Blockheads, The Stranglers and, of course, Roger Daltrey from The Who. He's also dabbled in acting and played a sinister part as an executioner in both the first and second series of *Game of Thrones*.

His distinctive sound is as a result of using his fingers to pluck the strings, instead of using a plectrum, as most guitarists do. I had no idea what to expect, but I don't like to miss out and Jeremy said I'd love it. We were going with Hammond too, which was a rare moment for those two to socialise outside of work. I was close to Richard and always enjoyed his company. I felt honoured to share the experience.

I was not disappointed, although I did feel slightly uncomfortable at first as, without exaggeration, I, as a woman, was outnumbered by ageing, grey, balding or bald old-man rockers by about 500 to one. I was soon distracted by the incredible performance from Wilko, who was very much celebrating being alive after a recent terminal cancer diagnosis. He and Roger Daltrey had arranged the night to raise funds for the Teenage Cancer Trust. At the same time they were clearly enjoying themselves.

Roger Daltrey was very amusing. Although he still looked amazing, with a good head of hair, and the ability to move in a rock-'n'-roll kind of way, he couldn't see or remember so well! He had to pause mid-set, don his glasses and check the set list and sometimes the lyrics whilst putting the heckling crowd in their place with a friendly 'Fu** you! You get up and try this.'

Wilko, however, did not put a finger wrong. I have never heard anything like it. Check him out on YouTube. Several years after his cancer diagnosis, he is still going very strong. A true rock-'n'-roller.

Talking of music and YouTube, you can also find a very inspiring version of 'Mustang Sally' on the social media giant, performed by the Fab Four, I mean the Terrible Three: Clarkson on drums, Hammond on base, and May on keyboards. Yours truly, along with Mindy Hammond and Gemma, head of marketing for *Top Gear Live*, give it our all as backing singers.

Our little performance was a surprise stitch-up for our gobby tour manager, Chris Hughes, who loved to sing, whether we liked it or not. Jeremy, James and Richard thought he might like to round off our twelve-year tour as lead singer in front of thousands at the O2. Jeremy called him, along with the rest of the crew, out on stage at the end of the final show for them to be applauded by the huge crowds. As Chris took the mic to say his thank-yous, a stage with keyboards, drums, bass and mics already set up was rolled out and Chris was actually speechless for just a little while before he belted out his favourite karaoke number.

*   *   *   *

It was a privilege being part of this celebrity, high-society world, where each high-profile personality helps to boost the others by inviting them to openings, launches, gigs and even fashion shows.

Jeremy was unable to attend, but I had the wonderful experience of my first high-profile fashion show put on by handbag designer Anya Hindmarch.

Anya is known for her quirky, childlike logos and accessories on her high-quality luxury bags. This particular season's show was inspired by the very uninspiring M25. Anya must be the only person to have gained from being stuck in traffic on London's notoriously bad ring road. The catwalk was turned into a highway, complete with overhead gantry signage.

The models were wearing utilitarian, workman-inspired clothing, as of course it was all about the bag. The bags were decorated with various nods to life on the motorway. Anya is known for her big tassels (on her bags, I mean) and sticker patches. Amongst this season's collection were classic roadworks triangle signs, Eddie Stobart logos, traffic-cone and bollard accessories, which add great, bright colours to liven up the most practical of bags. I actually loved the theme, being a big road-trip fan, and a bit tomboyish.

It was a shame Jeremy couldn't make it as of course it would have been a great PR stunt to have the King of Motoring attend the event. He would also have loved the Welsh choir that performed in the highest viz of roadside fashion, full orange ensembles were topped off with hard hats. The huge irony was I got caught up in traffic on my way to this literally traffic-stopping event.

Thank goodness I did get there in time to enjoy the singing finale and I have my handbag sticker patch from my invitation as a souvenir, now proudly placed on my Anya Hindmarch bag that Jeremy treated me to in one of his generous moments. It's the most apt sticker patch ever – a yellow rectangle with the familiar traffic message of 'Expect Severe Delays' – I am always late: something the big man despised and about which we often argued. Of course, my lateness was so often due to terrible traffic.

24

End of the Road

The last few outings with Jeremy were very emotional. Another one of his favourite musicians, Roger Hodgson, was playing at the Royal Albert Hall. Roger was one of the founding members and front men of rock band Supertramp. Roger composed and sang most of the band's hits. After over a decade of success with the band he had decided to go solo.

Jeremy and I had tickets arranged for us by the lovely Nick Allott, who had booked a box for a few of us. Both he and Christa were huge fans, too, and in the usual VIP way we were invited backstage to meet Roger in person. Jeremy was actually in awe of the man and loved discussing lyrics and where the inspiration for the music had come from.

The big man let his emotions show for a rare and raw moment as he sang along to 'Hide in Your Shell' and 'The Logical Song'. There's a real old soul buried deep behind his ridiculous façade, what the world sees of Mr Clarkson. I just wish he'd not sold himself out to the toxic world he was in.

Ooh, sorry, getting a bit soppy. And I'm only about to get more so.

Jeremy and I had reached the end of the road and sadly ended our relationship in a rather ugly way. However, through the terrible news of perhaps his closest friend, Adrian Gill, being diagnosed and very quickly hospitalised with terminal cancer, we were drawn back together again.

I had got close to Adrian as he had supported me during my relationship with Jeremy. Jeremy and I sought to reconcile and, even from his hospital bed, Adrian was trying to influence Jeremy for the better.

Jeremy got the news that Adrian had passed away after his very short battle while he was away filming and about to go out on set to film for the studio/tent of *The Grand Tour*. Even though our reconciliation had failed badly, Andy Wilman begged me to comfort Jeremy and support him with the immediate need to get him out in front of the live audience.

Jeremy dragged himself through filming and was planning to fly home immediately afterwards. Caught up in the grief and my continuing concerns for Jeremy, I arranged to meet him at Jemima Khan's London home, where he was going straight from the airport. Nicola, Adrian's now wife – they had got married just before he died – was being supported at Jemima's by a few of their closest friends at this terribly sad time.

* * * *

Adrian was known for his acerbic wit and often upset people with his very honest critiques. He was no stranger to the Press Complaints Commission. However, I knew him as a very caring friend of Jezza, an adoring partner of Nicola and an amazing, fun-loving and inspirational father, full of love for his four children.

Adrian was a real character, who had struggled with dyslexia through a troubled school life, which led him to bumble his way through a number of jobs and careers, including as an artist and a cookery teacher. As he discovered his talent for storytelling, he began to travel the world reporting on the plight of communities in war-torn countries. He also became *The Sunday Times* TV and restaurant critic and agony uncle for *GQ* magazine.

He had come a long way from one of his interim jobs as a shop assistant in a men's outfitters, (fashion was also a passion of his), which he became so bored with one day he decided to unwrap a pack of underpants and smear some chocolate in them before wrapping them back up and putting them back on display!! And now you know why Jeremy and he were such good friends.

It was heartbreaking to witness Adrian's grown-up children from his previous marriage to Amber Rudd (former home secretary) and the young twins he had with Nicola racked with grief.

Through Adrian's death, Jeremy and I were drawn back together. Through grief and the need for me to alleviate the pain that Jeremy was going through. Not only had he lost Adrian, but in a short space of time, he'd effectively lost me, his wife, his mother, his dream job at the BBC and, perhaps most importantly, his relationship with his children was severely fractured.

Just a few days after Adrian's passing, Jeremy was asked to stand in for him at a charity event for Nordoff Robbins, which raises money for music therapy to help children with autism, people living with dementia and those facing terminal illness.

It's a very high-profile charity, supported by the likes of Sir Paul McCartney, The Rolling Stones, Sir Elton John, Sir Cliff Richard and many other big names in music, along with other high-society brands such as *Tatler* magazine, The White Company and Theo Fennell jewellery – Theo is another one of Jeremy's contacts.

The event was a carol service in St Luke's Church, Chelsea, which would have fitted right in as a scene in *Love Actually* or *Last Christmas*. It's a beautiful church, which looks perfectly magical at Christmastime, decorated with Christmas trees adorned with lights.

Jeremy was understandably really nervous. He was to do a reading that Adrian had originally been booked to do. It was such an incredibly emotional event, as you might imagine, with many of Adrian's friends meeting for the first time since his death. Belle and Hamish were there, Nicola of course, Nick Allott and Christa, Michael Gambon and Philippa; Michael was also doing a reading.

The other celebs performing that night were Jenna Coleman, best known for *Emmerdale* and *Doctor Who*, Gillian Anderson, who I first knew and loved when she was in *The X-Files* – she is timeless and absolutely beautiful in the flesh and another friend of Jeremy.

I don't know how Jeremy got through it, but, ever the professional, he did. I found myself blubbing through most of the beautiful service. A death is always awful, but at Christmas, when young children have been left behind, like Adrian's were, it is heart-breaking.

There were incredible performances from the amazing duet, Ward Thomas and the fantastic Tom Odell, who broke me completely, emotionally. Aside from the terrible sadness of losing dear Adrian it was the best Christmas event I'd ever been to. (Apart from my son's first nativity, of course.) To be front row with these brilliant artists with the powerful acoustic setting of a church was awesome.

What a Christmas this one turned out to be.

The next event was Adrian's funeral, which was undoubtedly going to be extremely sad, but it was beautiful, even his coffin was. Adrian was a great nature lover, so it was fitting that he should be buried in a woven casket that was decorated with an explosion of flowers of all kinds and colours. And here's the first comedy moment: as Jeremy and I headed to our seats, Jimmy Carr and Caroline greeted us with a hug, then Jimmy quipped, 'Only Adrian would leave this world in a picnic basket,' obviously making reference to his job as a food critic. All the best funerals are a heady mix of tears and laughter.

The tragedy of this one was that Adrian had been to hell and back with personal suffering, no doubt contributing to his drink and drug addictions. He'd seen sense though, cleaned himself up and was leading a wonderful fulfilled life with his beloved family and entertaining the world with his genius writing. He had tragically been taken too soon.

The service was beautiful. All his children read, including the little ones, proving that the wonderful, eccentric, often offensive A A Gill was certainly leaving a mighty legacy behind in all of them.

Outside the church in London, which Adrian regularly attended and supported, the mourners gathered, and comedy moment number two played out. Since my big bust-up with Jeremy, I hadn't seen Nick Love and Alice B-B for months, and I had grown so close to them. They, too, had been very supportive during the ups and downs of my relationship with Jeremy.

When I saw Nick, I crumpled, sobbing uncontrollably. He gave me a hearty hug, engulfing me with his layers of cashmere (pyjamas and cashmere were Nick's staple wardrobe). He then said in his rough ol' cockney accent, 'All right, love, that's enough snotting all over me cashmere.' I went from tears to laughter and back again; that's what the whole day was like.

We all headed back to Jemima's London pad for the wake, and more laughter and tears. It was most strange as I had been off the scene for some months, but all the usual suspects were delighted to see me and hoped the big man and I could work things out.

Jeremy was rather embarrassingly telling everyone that Adrian's last words to him, from his deathbed were, 'Don't let go of Phillipa.' Wakes for relatively young people are so odd, as they are like a party with the guest of honour missing. Adrian would have loved it, being the centre of attention, being applauded and hailed by the great and the good.

Despite Adrian's advice, Jeremy did not want to calm his life down and, in fact, seemed to want to party and enjoy the high life even more than ever in true rock-'n'-roll fashion.

We finally closed the door on our relationship in 2017. I had had the most amazing time on this crazy roller-coaster existence, but I couldn't keep up with Mr Clarkson in the fast lane of his extraordinary life.

Jezza, thanks for the ride.